THE
soups and
stews
COOKBOOK

A SOUTHERN LIVING BOOK

contents

preface

Versatile soups and stews can be whatever we want them to be. They can be simple or dramatic, served anytime of the day or during any course of the meal. This *Soups and Stews Cookbook* is designed to provide you with hundreds of choices of appetizer, main dish, or dessert soups for party or family fare.

When a meal begins with soup, dinner naturally takes on a more gracious and formal atmosphere. Light soups (broths and creams) make delightful appetizers when served hot or chilled.

A hearty soup or stew can be a meal in itself for lunch or supper. These are usually made with meat, poultry, or seafood with the addition of vegetables, rice, or pasta. You can make these as rich or nourishing as you want them to be. Hot and hearty soups or stews are the best warm-up foods you can expect to eat on a cold day. We suggest other variations of these hearty dishes in our selection of chowder, gumbo, and chili recipes.

Hot or cold fruit soups make refreshing and unusual desserts or appetizers. These can be made from an array of fresh, dried, or canned fruits.

The following collection of recipes presents a variety of long-time favorite as well as new soups and stews. We hope also to give you some novel ideas for putting soup on your table anytime of the day.

broths

Broth is a thin liquid in which meat, poultry, and vegetables or any combination of these has been cooked. These delicate soups form the base for a variety of sauces, gravies, other soups, and even some recipes requiring a flavorful liquid to bind various ingredients.

A broth may be thickened with rice or barley or made richer by allowing it to simmer for a longer period than stated; reducing the broth concentrates the flavor. When additional vegetables or cereal are added to broth, it can be a substantial meal if a potato, salad, and bread are added to make a complete menu.

Broth is perishable and should be used within three or four days; however, that's no reason not to make a large supply. We recommend that broth and stock be frozen in containers of a variety of sizes—anything from a cup to a quart. It is also handy to freeze broth in ice cube trays and transfer the cubes to a plastic bag for freezer storage. (Each small cube yields about 2 tablespoons.)

One tip to remember when making broth: allow sufficient time for the broth to cool before using. The fat will rise to the surface and become firm. This layer can be lifted off and makes for a healthier, lighter broth. Chilling is the most effective way of degreasing broth or stock, but if time is limited, wrap an ice cube in cheesecloth and skim it over the surface. The fat will congeal on contact with the ice and can easily be lifted off. Also, a bulb baster can be used to lift fat off the top of broth and stock.

ALMOND SOUP

1 cup chopped onion
3 tablespoons melted butter or
  margarine
2 quarts chicken broth
½ cup uncooked regular rice
1 teaspoon salt
½ teaspoon pepper

½ teaspoon saffron
1 cup finely ground blanched
  almonds
3 hard-cooked egg yolks,
  finely chopped
3 tablespoons minced parsley

Sauté onion in butter until golden; stir in broth, and bring to a boil. Cover and simmer 10 minutes. Stir in rice, salt, pepper, and saffron; simmer 20 additional minutes. Add almonds, egg yolks, and parsley; cook 10 minutes longer. Yield: 10 servings.

Photograph for this recipe on page 6

EGG NOODLE SOUP

1 quart beef or chicken broth
  (See Index)
4 eggs

1 tablespoon parsley flakes
Salt and pepper to taste
Croutons

Simmer broth in large saucepan. Beat eggs with a fork until yolks and whites are thoroughly blended. Slowly pour eggs into broth, stirring with fork. The eggs form noodlelike strands when cooked. Add parsley flakes, salt, and pepper and let simmer for 10 minutes. Serve hot with croutons. Yield: 4 to 5 servings.

QUICK EGG DROP SOUP

1 (2¼-ounce) envelope
  dehydrated chicken noodle
  soup mix
4 to 6 fresh mushrooms, thinly
  sliced

1 teaspoon chopped parsley
1 egg, well beaten

Prepare soup mix according to package directions. Add mushrooms and parsley, and cook for 5 minutes. Slowly add egg, stirring constantly. Serve as a first course for a Chinese dinner. Yield: 4 to 6 servings.

■ *Cooking vegetables with the least amount of water possible will preserve vitamins and maintain flavor. Save the cooking liquid, and add to soup stock or gravy for additional food value and flavor.*

QUICK JELLIED MADRILÈNE

2 envelopes unflavored gelatin
1 cup cold water
2 beef bouillon cubes
2 chicken bouillon cubes
2 cups hot water

2 (8-ounce) cans tomato
   sauce
2 tablespoons lemon juice
Lemon slices

Soften gelatin in cold water. Dissolve beef and chicken bouillon cubes in hot water; add to softened gelatin, and stir until dissolved. Stir in tomato sauce and lemon juice. Pour into shallow pan; chill until firm. To serve, cut into cubes, or spoon into soup cups. Top each cup with a slice of lemon. Yield: 8 servings.

MADRILÈNE WITH CLAMS

2 (8-ounce) cartons
   commercial sour cream
2 (10-ounce) cans Madrilène
   (jellied consommé)
1 teaspoon salt
½ teaspoon freshly ground
   black pepper
1 tablespoon minced chives

2 tablespoons lemon or lime
   juice
2 (8-ounce) cans clams,
   drained
Commercial sour cream
   (optional)
Red caviar (optional)

Whip sour cream into consommé with rotary beater until mixture is smooth and thickened. Fold in seasonings, chives, lemon juice, and clams. Check seasonings and chill until serving time. Garnish with more minced chives or with a tablespoon of sour cream topped with ½ teaspoon of red caviar, if desired. Yield: 8 servings.

BEEF BROTH

2½ pounds cut-up beef shanks
2 quarts water
1 carrot, cut into eighths
1 onion, quartered
2 stalks celery

1 bay leaf
2 cloves garlic
¼ teaspoon thyme
Salt and pepper to taste

Roast meat at 400° for 20 minutes or until browned. Transfer meat to a large kettle and add remaining ingredients. Bring to a boil and simmer, covered, for 2 hours. Strain broth; reserve meat and vegetables for other uses. Cool and skim off fat. Cover and store in refrigerator until ready to use. Yield: about 1½ quarts.

Note: Canned beef broth, beef broth made with bouillon cubes, or beef concentrate may be substituted for freshly made beef broth.

BULL SHOT SOUP

1 (10½-ounce) can condensed beef broth, undiluted	½ soup can water
	½ cup vodka

Heat broth and water just to boil. Stir in vodka. Yield: 3 servings.

HAM STOCK

2 pounds ham and ham bone	1 stalk celery, coarsely diced
5 cups water	½ teaspoon dried parsley
1 carrot, sliced	½ bay leaf
1 onion, quartered	

Combine all ingredients in a kettle; cover and simmer 30 to 40 minutes. Strain broth; discard residue. Cool and skim off fat. Cover and store in refrigerator until ready to use. Yield: about 1 quart.

SCOTCH BROTH

Bones and trimmings from lamb roast	3 carrots, chopped
3 quarts water	2 onions, chopped
½ teaspoon pepper	1½ cups chopped celery and leaves
½ cup barley	¼ cup chopped parsley
1 cup dried split peas	Salt and pepper to taste

Put bones and trimmings into soup kettle; add water, pepper, and barley; let stand 1 hour. Add split peas; bring to a boil slowly and skim. Simmer about 2 hours or until barley is tender. Remove bones; mince any bits of meat on bones to add to soup; cool soup and remove fat. Add carrots, onions, and celery; simmer 1 hour. Add parsley; season with salt and pepper. Simmer for 5 minutes. Yield: 3 quarts.

CHICKEN BROTH

4 pounds chicken pieces	¼ teaspoon thyme
1 onion, quartered	⅛ teaspoon marjoram
2 stalks celery	2 quarts water
½ teaspoon dried parsley	Salt and pepper to taste
1 bay leaf	

Combine chicken and remaining ingredients in a large kettle. Cover and bring to a boil; reduce heat and simmer 3 hours or until meat falls from bones. Strain broth; reserve chicken and vegetables for other uses. Cool and skim off fat. Cover and store in refrigerator until ready to use. Yield: about 1½ quarts.

Note: Canned chicken broth, chicken broth made with bouillon cubes, or chicken concentrate may be substituted for freshly made chicken broth. Also, turkey pieces may be substituted for chicken in the above recipe to make turkey broth.

CHICKEN BROTH WITH MUSHROOMS AND ALMONDS

2 quarts chicken broth (See
   Index)
½ teaspoon oregano
1½ cups chopped mushrooms
2 tablespoons lemon juice

Salt and pepper to taste
¼ cup toasted slivered
   almonds
2 tablespoons chopped fresh
   chervil

Skim all fat from chicken broth and simmer with oregano and mushrooms about 10 minutes. Add lemon juice, salt, pepper, almonds, and chervil. Serve immediately. Yield: 8 servings.

CONSOMMÉ ROUGE

1 medium onion, cut in half
   and sliced paper-thin
2 small beets, peeled
1 teaspoon salt

1½ teaspoons red wine
1 quart rich chicken broth,
   skimmed of all fat (See
   Index)

Cook sliced onion until soft in large saucepan in water to cover. Pour off liquid; grate beets into the saucepan; add salt, wine, and chicken broth. Bring to a boil, reduce heat, and simmer uncovered for 25 minutes. Remove from heat and strain. Yield: 6 servings.

CLAM AND TOMATO BROTH WITH TARRAGON

2 cups clam juice   2 teaspoons fresh tarragon
2 cups tomato juice

Heat all ingredients and strain. Serve hot. Yield: 6 servings.

FISH STOCK

2 pounds fish bones or heads   ⅓ cup sliced celery
5 cups water   ½ bay leaf
⅓ cup sliced carrot   ½ teaspoon dried parsley
⅓ cup sliced onion   Salt and pepper to taste

Combine all ingredients in a kettle; cover and simmer 30 minutes. Strain broth; discard residue. Cool and skim off fat. Cover and store in refrigerator until ready to use. Yield: 1 quart.

CLEAR TOMATO SOUP

2 (46-ounce) cans tomato   2 bay leaves
   juice   6 peppercorns
1 beef bouillon cube for each   2 thick slices onion
   2 cups liquid   Parsley
4 stalks celery with leaves,   Commercial sour cream
   chopped   Chopped chives

Combine all ingredients except sour cream and chives in large soup kettle. Cover and simmer for 2 hours over low heat. Strain; check seasonings and serve with a dollop of sour cream combined with chives. Yield: 10 to 12 servings.

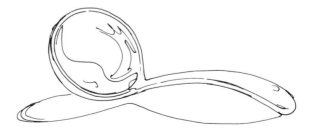

▪ *For a quick way to peel tomatoes, hold tomato over flame or heat for 1 minute.*

HOT TOMATO BOUILLON

1 (10-ounce) can bouillon,
   undiluted
2 cups tomato juice
1 teaspoon Worcestershire
   sauce

8 paper-thin slices lemon
   (optional)

Combine bouillon, juice, and Worcestershire sauce in saucepan, and bring
to boiling point. Serve in mugs; garnish with lemon slice on top, if desired.
Yield: 4 or 5 servings.

LETTUCE SOUP

1 (10½-ounce) can condensed
   consommé, undiluted
1 cup water

2 cups shredded lettuce
1 teaspoon wine vinegar

Heat consommé with water. Add lettuce and vinegar just before serving.
Heat just enough to wilt lettuce; serve hot. Yield: 3 to 4 servings.

WATERCRESS SOUP

1 bunch watercress
2 (10½-ounce) cans
   condensed consommé,
   undiluted

2 teaspoons all-purpose flour
2 teaspoons melted butter or
   margarine

Put watercress through meat chopper, using finest blade. Heat consommé;
add watercress. Combine flour and butter; add to consommé. Serve
immediately. Yield: 6 servings.

chilies

While it is generally believed that chili is a Mexican import, the fact is that this spicy dish really had its origin almost 100 years ago in San Antonio. And in Texas, where almost all Texans love their "bowl of red," there are as many variations of chili as there are cooks. It's not surprising then that each fall the Chili Appreciation Society hosts the International Chili Cook-Off near Terlingua, Texas, to temporarily settle which chili is truly the best.

The two hottest conflicts in chili cooking concern the use of ground beef versus chunks of beef and the addition of beans. As long as chili lovers are devouring the fiery stuff, we'll never finally resolve which is better—chili con carne (chili with meat) or chili con frijoles (chili with beans).

For you to choose your favorite chili, we have selected recipes reflecting a variety of tastes. You can savor chili using ground beef and pork, chunks of beef, and chili with or without beans. For the hunters among you, we've even included a recipe featuring venison.

Although you may not have considered chili as party fare, it's an ideal main dish for informal suppers. Put out a steaming pot of chili and let your guests create a bowl of red to their own liking with various condiments. Set out bowls of shredded lettuce, shredded Cheddar cheese, diced onion, and tortilla chips. And for the real chili fiends, pass the chili powder.

SAVORY CHILI

¼ cup olive oil
2 cloves garlic, minced
1 large onion, chopped
3 green onions, chopped
4 stalks celery with leaves,
   chopped
1 tablespoon chopped parsley
2 pounds ground chuck
1 (6-ounce) can tomato paste
1 (15-ounce) can tomato
   sauce

5 to 6 cups water
1 (1½-ounce) can chili
   powder
1¼ teaspoons salt
Dash of pepper
1 cup cooked red beans
   (optional)
Condiments

Heat olive oil in a 5-quart Dutch oven. Add garlic, onion, celery, and parsley; sauté just until tender, about 5 minutes. Add ground beef, and brown, stirring occasionally.

Drain off pan drippings, reserving 3 tablespoons. Add reserved pan drippings to meat mixture. Stir in tomato paste, tomato sauce, water, chili powder, salt, and pepper. Bring to a boil; reduce heat, and simmer 1 hour. Add red beans during last 15 minutes, if desired.

Serve chili with the following condiments: shredded lettuce, shredded Cheddar cheese, diced onion, and tortilla chips. Yield: 8 to 10 servings.

Photograph for this recipe on page 14

CHILI CON CARNE FOR A CROWD

5 pounds ground beef
2½ tablespoons salt
½ teaspoon pepper
⅓ cup salad oil, divided
2½ cups chopped onion
6 (16-ounce) cans kidney
   beans

3 (28-ounce) cans whole
   tomatoes
5 tablespoons chili powder
12 cups hot cooked rice
1½ cups coarsely shredded
   Cheddar cheese

Season meat with salt and pepper; sauté about 1 pound of meat at a time in 1 tablespoon oil in large skillet. Place meat in large pan. Sauté onion in drippings in skillet until tender but not browned. Add to meat. Add remaining ingredients except rice and cheese and stir well. Bring to a boil, cover, reduce heat, and simmer about 45 minutes. Serve in soup bowls over hot rice. Sprinkle with shredded cheese. Yield: 24 servings.

CHILI WITH BEANS

¾ teaspoon minced garlic
1 teaspoon water
1 tablespoon salad oil
2 pounds ground chuck
2 tablespoons chili powder
2½ teaspoons salt
1½ teaspoons cumin seeds

2 (16-ounce) cans whole
   tomatoes
¼ cup tomato paste
½ teaspoon sugar
1 (16-ounce) can kidney
   beans, drained

Soften garlic in 1 teaspoon water. Put, undrained, into kettle with oil and sauté for 1 to 2 minutes. Add meat and cook, stirring frequently, until beef loses its red color. Stir in chili powder, salt, cumin, and tomatoes. Bring to a boil and simmer, uncovered, for 25 minutes. Add tomato paste and sugar; simmer for 15 minutes. Add beans and heat. Yield: 6 servings.

HEARTY BAKED CHILI AND BEANS

5 cups water
2 teaspoons salt
1 pound dried pinto beans,
   washed
2 pounds ground beef
1 (28-ounce) can whole
   tomatoes
2 medium onions, chopped

1 clove garlic, minced
¼ cup chili powder
1 tablespoon salt
¼ teaspoon ground cumin
¼ teaspoon pepper

Bring water and salt to a boil in a Dutch oven; add beans, return to a boil, and boil 2 minutes. Remove from heat; cover and let soak 1 hour.

Brown beef in a skillet; add to beans. Stir in remaining ingredients; cover and bake at 350° for 3½ hours or until beans are tender. Remove cover, and bake 30 minutes longer. Yield: about 8 servings.

SUPER HOT AND SPICY CHILI

¼ pound dried pinto beans
Water
2 (10-ounce) cans tomatoes
　with chilies
¼ cup margarine
1¼ pounds ground beef
½ pound ground pork
1¾ cups chopped green
　pepper
1 tablespoon salad oil

2½ cups chopped onion
¼ cup chopped parsley
1 clove garlic, crushed
3 to 4 tablespoons chili
　powder
1 tablespoon salt
1 teaspoon pepper
1 teaspoon cumin seeds
1 teaspoon monosodium
　glutamate

Wash beans; cover with 2 inches water in a large Dutch oven, and soak overnight. Cook beans in same water, covered, until tender. Add tomatoes; simmer 5 minutes.

Melt ¼ cup margarine in 10-inch skillet. Add meat; cook until browned. Set aside.

Sauté green pepper in oil 5 minutes; add onion and cook until tender. Stir in meat mixture, parsley, garlic, and chili powder; cook 10 minutes over low heat. Add mixture to beans; stir in remaining ingredients. Cover and simmer 1 hour; uncover and simmer 30 minutes longer. Yield: 8 to 10 servings.

GEORGIA CHILI

1 pound ground beef
Salt and pepper to taste
3 tablespoons chili powder,
　divided
1 onion, chopped
1 tablespoon shortening
2 cups tomato juice or water

2 stalks celery, diced
1 green pepper, diced
1 (16-ounce) can whole
　tomatoes
1 (16-ounce) can kidney
　beans

Season ground beef with salt, pepper, and 1 tablespoon chili powder. Brown beef and onion in shortening. Add tomato juice, celery, green pepper, and remaining 2 tablespoons chili powder. Simmer slowly for 45 minutes or until vegetables are tender. (If mixture cooks down, add more tomato juice or water.) Add tomatoes and simmer 15 minutes longer; then add kidney beans and simmer a few minutes more. Yield: 6 servings.

CALEB'S CHILI

9 pounds chuck roast
¼ cup salad oil
15 cloves garlic, minced
5 large onions, finely chopped
2½ quarts hot water
¾ cup chili powder
1 tablespoon ground oregano
2 tablespoons ground cumin

3 tablespoons salt
6 jalapeño peppers, finely
　chopped
2 squares unsweetened
　chocolate
2 tablespoons masa harina
½ cup cold water

Cut meat into small pieces and cook in hot oil until meat turns white. Add garlic, onions, and hot water; cover and simmer for 1 hour or until meat is tender.

Add chili powder, oregano, cumin, and salt; cook slowly for another hour, stirring occasionally. Add additional water, if needed. Taste and add more seasoning, if needed. Add peppers and chocolate, and stir until chocolate is dissolved. Stir masa harina (a corn flour; cornmeal can be substituted) into cold water; add to chili and cook and stir until mixture thickens. Serve hot. Yield: 12 to 16 servings.

CHAMPIONSHIP CHILI

2 large onions, chopped	1 (1½-ounce) can chili powder
3 cloves garlic, minced	1 (28-ounce) can whole tomatoes
1 jalapeño pepper, finely chopped	3½ cups water
1 tablespoon peanut oil	1½ teaspoons instant corn masa (optional)
3 pounds boneless chuck roast, finely diced	Shredded Cheddar cheese (optional)
1 teaspoon cumin seeds	
1½ tablespoons oregano	

Sauté onion, garlic, and jalapeño pepper in oil until tender; set aside. Combine meat, cumin, and oregano in a Dutch oven; cook until meat is browned. Add onion mixture, chili powder, tomatoes, and water; bring to a boil. Reduce heat and simmer 2 to 3 hours, stirring frequently.

For thicker chili, combine corn masa with small amount of cold water to make a paste; add to chili, stirring constantly. Top with shredded cheese, if desired. Yield: 5 to 7 servings.

CHILI WITH BEEF CUBES

¼ cup finely chopped beef suet	1 clove garlic, crushed
1¼ pounds beef round steak, cut in 1-inch squares	1½ teaspoons dark brown sugar
2 medium onions, chopped	1½ teaspoons chili powder
3 medium tomatoes, peeled and quartered	1½ teaspoons red wine vinegar
½ cup water	Salt and pepper to taste

Melt suet in a 10-inch skillet; add beef and onion, and cook until meat is browned. Stir in remaining ingredients; cover and simmer 1½ hours or until meat is tender. Yield: 3 to 4 servings.

CHILI CON CARNE

1 pound beef stew meat, cut into ½-inch cubes	4 teaspoons chili powder
1 tablespoon butter or margarine	¼ teaspoon garlic powder
⅔ cup chopped onion	¼ teaspoon freshly ground black pepper
¼ cup chopped green pepper	2 cups canned whole tomatoes
1 tablespoon salt	1 (16-ounce) can red kidney beans
1 teaspoon sugar	4 cups hot cooked rice

Combine meat, butter, onion, and green pepper in saucepan; cook, uncovered, until mixture sizzles, about 10 minutes. Add seasonings and tomatoes. Cover. Simmer about 1 hour or until meat is tender. Add kidney beans and heat. Serve over cooked rice. Yield: 6 servings.

HOMEMADE CHILI

3 pounds chuck or round steak	1 teaspoon ground oregano
2 tablespoons salad oil	2 teaspoons ground cumin
2 large onions, chopped	2 tablespoons salt
2 to 3 cloves garlic, minced	2 jalapeño peppers, finely chopped
3 cups hot water	Cooked pinto beans (optional)
2 to 4 tablespoons chili powder	

Cut meat into small pieces and fry in hot oil until fully cooked. Add onions, garlic, and hot water; cover and simmer for 1 hour or until meat is tender.

Add chili powder, oregano, cumin, salt, and peppers; cook slowly for another hour, stirring occasionally. Add additional hot water, if needed. Taste and add more seasoning, if needed. Serve hot, with cooked pinto beans, if desired. Yield: 8 to 10 servings.

TEXAS CHILI

12 pounds chuck roast	2 tablespoons fresh oregano, crushed
½ cup salad oil	¼ cup salt
15 to 20 cloves garlic, crushed	1 (4-ounce) can green chilies, chopped
8 large onions, chopped	2 tablespoons all-purpose flour
3 quarts hot water	½ cup cold water
¾ to 1 cup chili powder	
1 tablespoon ground cumin	

Cut meat into small cubes, removing most of the fat and all of the gristle. Sauté in hot oil in a large skillet until meat turns white. Add garlic, onions, and hot water; cover pot and simmer for 1 hour or until meat is tender.

Add chili powder, cumin, oregano, and salt. Cook slowly for another hour, stirring occasionally. Add additional water if needed. Add chopped chilies; taste and add more seasoning, if needed. Stir flour into ½ cup cold water; add to chili mixture, and stir and cook until mixture is thick and clear. Serve hot. Yield: 16 to 20 servings.

VENISON CHILI

2 pounds venison, finely diced
1 tablespoon bacon drippings
2 tablespoons chili powder
1 teaspoon sage
⅛ teaspoon pepper
1 teaspoon salt
1 teaspoon ground cumin
2 onions, diced
2 cloves garlic, diced
2 (15-ounce) cans
  Spanish-style tomato sauce

2 cups water
1 (23-ounce) can ranch-style
  beans
Shredded lettuce
Shredded Cheddar cheese
Tortilla chips
Diced onion
Chili powder

Brown venison in bacon drippings; add chili powder, sage, pepper, salt, cumin, onions, and garlic. Stir in tomato sauce, water, and beans; simmer for 1 hour.

Serve chili with the following condiments: shredded lettuce, shredded Cheddar cheese, tortilla chips, diced onion, and chili powder. Yield: 6 servings.

chowders

Hot chowder is one of the best warmup foods you could serve on a cold day. In fact, nothing will please a family's appetite more on a winter day than the rich and warming goodness of a pot of homemade chowder.

Chowders probably originated on the shores of New England where seafood was plentiful. While today's chowders are still often laden with seafood, many recipes feature vegetables as the main ingredient.

Personal preference usually dictates whether a milk or tomato base is favored. A New England chowder is recognized by its creamy milk base, whereas a Manhattan chowder boasts a flavorful and perhaps less fattening tomato base.

CHEESE CHOWDER

2 slices bacon, diced
1 cup coarsely chopped onion
⅓ cup chopped celery
2 tablespoons all-purpose flour

1 teaspoon salt
3 cups milk
¾ cup shredded pasteurized
    process American cheese

Cook bacon until just crisp; add onion and celery and cook until tender. Stir in flour and salt. Gradually add milk. Cook over low heat until smooth and thickened, about 10 minutes. Stir often. Add cheese and stir until melted. Yield: 4 servings.

HOT CHEESE CHOWDER

3 cups canned chicken broth
¾ cup finely chopped carrot
½ cup finely chopped onion
1 cup finely chopped celery
¼ cup melted butter or
    margarine
¼ cup all-purpose flour

¼ teaspoon salt
⅛ teaspoon paprika
2 cups milk
½ pound sharp Cheddar
    cheese, shredded
1 tablespoon prepared mustard
¼ cup finely snipped parsley

Simmer chicken broth and carrot, covered, in saucepan for about 15 minutes or until carrot is tender. Sauté onion and celery in butter until tender and golden. Remove from heat; stir in flour, salt, paprika, and milk. Bring to a boil, stirring, until mixture is thickened and smooth. Stir in chicken broth with carrot, cheese, and mustard. Heat until cheese is melted. Garnish with parsley. Yield: 8 servings.

HEARTY CHEDDAR CHOWDER

3 cups water
3 chicken bouillon cubes
4 medium potatoes, peeled
    and diced
1 medium onion, sliced
1 cup thinly sliced carrots
½ cup diced green pepper
⅓ cup butter or margarine

⅓ cup all-purpose flour
3½ cups milk
4 cups shredded sharp
    Cheddar cheese
1 (2-ounce) jar diced
    pimiento, drained
¼ teaspoon hot sauce
    (optional)

Combine water and bouillon cubes in a Dutch oven; bring to a boil. Add vegetables; cover and simmer 12 minutes or until vegetables are tender.

Melt butter in a heavy saucepan; blend in flour, and cook 1 minute. Gradually add milk; cook over medium heat until thickened, stirring constantly. Add cheese, stirring until melted.

Stir cheese sauce, pimiento, and hot sauce into vegetable mixture. Cook over low heat until thoroughly heated (do not boil). Yield: 8 to 10 servings.

Photograph for this recipe on page 22

CHEESE-CORN CHOWDER

¼ cup butter
¼ cup chopped onion
¼ cup all-purpose flour
1 quart milk
2 (16-ounce) cans cream-style
    corn

2 cups shredded sharp
    pasteurized process
    American cheese
2 teaspoons salt
¼ teaspoon pepper
Chopped fresh parsley

Melt butter in saucepan over low heat; sauté onion in butter until transparent but not brown (approximately 5 minutes) Add flour and blend thoroughly. Add milk slowly while stirring constantly; cook mixture until smooth and thickened. Stir in corn and cheese, heat until cheese melts, do not boil. Add seasonings. Serve sprinkled with parsley. Yield: 6 to 8 servings.

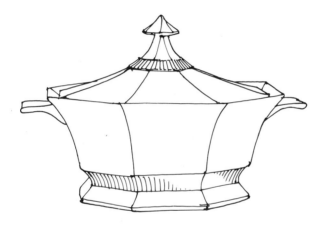

MEATBALL CHOWDER

½ cup breadcrumbs
½ cup milk
1 pound beef
½ pound pork
½ pound veal
1 cup diced potatoes
½ cup diced celery
1 egg
1 teaspoon salt
⅛ teaspoon ground nutmeg
¼ cup chopped onion

¼ teaspoon pepper
¼ teaspoon brown sugar
⅛ teaspoon ground allspice
2 tablespoons shortening
1 (10½-ounce) can tomato
    soup, undiluted
1 cup water
1 cup diced potatoes
1 cup cut green beans
½ cup diced celery

Soak breadcrumbs in the milk. Grind beef, pork, veal, 1 cup potatoes, and ½ cup celery. Add soaked breadcrumbs, and mix thoroughly. Add the egg, salt, nutmeg, onion, pepper, brown sugar, and allspice, and shape into balls no larger than 1 inch in diameter. Brown in hot shortening. Add the soup, water, potatoes, green beans, and celery. Simmer until vegetables are cooked. Yield: 6 to 8 servings.

CHILI CHOWDER

1 pound ground chuck	1 soup can water
1 large onion, sliced	1 cup catsup
1 clove garlic, minced	¼ cup steak sauce
¼ cup melted margarine or butter	1 teaspoon salt
	¼ teaspoon pepper
1 (15½-ounce) can Mexican-style chili beans	½ teaspoon chili powder
	3 tablespoons honey
¼ chili bean can of water	½ lemon, sliced
1 (10¾-ounce) can condensed tomato soup, undiluted	

Brown meat, onion, and garlic in margarine over low heat. Add remaining ingredients and simmer for 20 minutes. Remove lemon slices and serve. Yield: 6 servings.

CORNED BEEF CHOWDER

1 (10¾-ounce) can condensed cream of potato soup, undiluted	Dash of pepper
	1 (12-ounce) can corned beef, broken into pieces
3 cups milk, divided	
1 (10-ounce) package frozen Brussels sprouts, thawed and quartered	

Combine soup and 1⅓ cups milk in a large saucepan. Stir in Brussels sprouts and pepper. Bring to boiling, stirring occasionally. Reduce heat; simmer for 15 minutes or until sprouts are tender. Add remaining 1⅔ cups milk and corned beef. Heat thoroughly. Yield: 4 to 5 servings.

HAM CHOWDER

1 (11½-ounce) can condensed split pea soup, undiluted	1½ cups cubed ham
½ teaspoon celery salt	1 hard-cooked egg, chopped
½ teaspoon seasoned salt	Shredded Cheddar cheese
1 (10-ounce) package frozen green lima beans or 1 (8-ounce) can green lima beans	Chinese noodles

Heat soup over boiling water in the top part of a double boiler. When hot, add celery salt, seasoned salt, lima beans, ham, and egg. Heat thoroughly, stirring to blend well. Serve in warm bowls, and offer a choice of shredded Cheddar cheese or Chinese noodle toppings. Yield: about 4 servings.

HAM AND CORN CHOWDER

3 slices bacon, chopped
2 medium onions, chopped
1 cup diced celery
2 tablespoons all-purpose flour
2 (13¾-ounce) cans chicken
   broth, undiluted
4 medium potatoes, diced

1 (10-ounce) package frozen
   whole kernel corn
3 cups milk
2 cups cubed cooked smoked
   ham
1 teaspoon salt
⅛ teaspoon pepper

Fry bacon until crisp. Add onion and celery, and sauté until golden brown. Sprinkle with flour, blending well; gradually stir in chicken broth. Add potatoes; cover and simmer until potatoes are done. Stir in remaining ingredients. Heat thoroughly, but do not boil. Yield: 8 to 10 servings.

SAUSAGE-BEAN CHOWDER

1 pound bulk hot pork
   sausage
2 (16-ounce) cans kidney
   beans, undrained
2 (14½-ounce) cans stewed
   tomatoes, undrained
2 cups tomato juice
1 large onion, chopped
1 bay leaf

1½ teaspoons seasoned salt
½ teaspoon garlic salt
1 teaspoon chili powder
½ teaspoon thyme
¼ teaspoon pepper
1 cup whole kernel corn
1 stalk celery, chopped
1 green pepper, chopped

Brown sausage; drain. Combine all ingredients in a large kettle. Simmer, covered, for 1 hour. Remove bay leaf. Serve hot. Yield: 10 to 12 servings.

SUCCOTASH AND HOT DOG CHOWDER

1 quart milk
1 (17-ounce) can cream-style
   corn
1 (10-ounce) package frozen
   lima beans
1 small onion, minced
1 teaspoon salt

⅓ teaspoon pepper
2 tablespoons cornstarch
¼ cup cold water
1 (1-pound) package wieners,
   sliced
½ cup shredded pasteurized
   process American cheese

Combine milk, corn, lima beans, onion, and seasonings; simmer for 15 minutes, stirring occasionally. Blend cornstarch and water; stir into succotash mixture. Add wieners. Cook, stirring frequently, until mixture thickens. Serve hot; sprinkle with cheese. Yield: 8 servings.

BRUNSWICK BREAKFAST CHOWDER

2 (10¾-ounce) cans
   condensed cream of
   chicken soup, undiluted
1½ soup cans milk
1 (6-ounce) can chicken,
   chopped
1 (12-ounce) can whole
   kernel corn, drained

1 (16-ounce) can whole
   tomatoes, drained and
   coarsely chopped
Salt and pepper to taste
Chopped pimiento
Chopped green pepper

Combine soup and milk; heat to simmering. Add chicken, corn, and tomatoes. Heat thoroughly, but do not allow to boil. Season. Garnish with pimiento and green pepper. Yield: 6 to 8 servings.

CHICKEN CHOWDER

1 (4-pound) roasting chicken,
    cut up
¼ teaspoon thyme
¼ teaspoon sage leaves
1 tablespoon salt
½ teaspoon pepper
3 medium onions, chopped
5 medium potatoes, diced

½ cup butter or margarine
⅓ cup all-purpose flour
2 cups milk
1 cup half-and-half
4 slices bacon, fried crisp and
    crumbled
Chopped parsley

Put chicken in kettle and cover with water; add herbs, salt, pepper, and onions. Bring to boil; cover and simmer for 1 hour or until chicken is tender. Remove chicken and take meat from bones. Add potatoes to broth and simmer, covered, for 15 minutes, or until potatoes are tender. Melt butter and blend in flour. Stir into soup and cook, stirring, until slightly thickened. Add chicken, milk, and half-and-half; heat. Serve sprinkled with bacon and parsley. Yield: 6 servings.

CHICKEN AND CORN CHOWDER

3 tablespoons chopped onion
2 tablespoons melted butter or
    margarine
1 (10¾-ounce) can condensed
    cream of celery soup,
    undiluted
1 (10¾-ounce) can condensed
    chicken-noodle soup,
    undiluted

1 soup can water
1 (12-ounce) can whole
    kernel corn, undrained
⅛ teaspoon pepper
Oyster crackers
Snipped parsley

Sauté onion in butter in saucepan until golden. Stir in soups, water, corn, and pepper. Bring to boil; simmer, stirring, about 5 minutes. Serve in mugs; top each serving with oyster crackers and parsley. Yield: 6 servings.

CATFISH CHOWDER

1 pound catfish fillets, fresh or
    frozen
½ cup chopped onion
2 tablespoons melted
    shortening
2 cups chopped potatoes

1 cup boiling water
¾ teaspoon salt
Pepper to taste
2 cups milk
1 (8¾-ounce) can cream-style
    corn

Thaw frozen fillets; remove skin, and cut fish into 1-inch squares.

Sauté onion in melted shortening until soft; add potatoes, water, salt, pepper, and fish. Cover and simmer 15 minutes or until potatoes are tender. Add milk and corn; heat thoroughly. Serve immediately. Yield: 6 servings.

FISH CHOWDER

2 tablespoons chopped onion
1 tablespoon melted butter or
  margarine
1 (10¾-ounce) can condensed
  cream of celery soup,
  undiluted
1 (10¾-ounce) can condensed
  clam chowder, undiluted

2½ cups milk
¼ teaspoon savory
2 cups diced raw fish
1 (16-ounce) can whole
  tomatoes, undrained
2 tablespoons chopped parsley

Sauté onion in butter in a large saucepan until tender. Add soups, milk, and savory. Bring to a boil; add fish and simmer for 10 to 15 minutes. Add tomatoes and parsley and heat thoroughly. Yield: 8 to 10 servings.

CREAMY FISH CHOWDER

1 cup diced potatoes
1 cup boiling water
3 slices bacon, chopped
1 medium onion, chopped
¾ pound fish fillets, cubed

1 cup milk
½ teaspoon salt
⅛ teaspoon pepper
2 tablespoons chopped fresh
  parsley

Place potatoes in boiling water in a Dutch oven; cover and cook 10 to 15 minutes. Fry bacon until transparent; add onion, and cook until onion is soft and bacon is lightly browned. Add bacon, onion, bacon drippings, and fish fillets to potatoes. Simmer 10 minutes or until potatoes and fish are done. Stir in milk, salt, and pepper; simmer 5 minutes. Sprinkle with parsley. Yield: 2 to 3 servings.

NEW ENGLAND FISH CHOWDER

¾ pound diced salt pork
2 large onions, sliced
3 cups diced potatoes
1 cup water
2 pounds fresh or thawed
  frozen haddock filets, diced

1 quart milk
1 tablespoon Worcestershire
  sauce
Salt and pepper to taste

Cook salt pork in large pan until lightly browned. Add onions and cook 5 minutes. Stir in potatoes and water. Cover and cook 15 minutes. Add remaining ingredients and mix well. Cover and cook over very low heat for 30 minutes, stirring occasionally. Yield: 6 to 8 servings.

CLAM CHOWDER AU VIN

2 cups diced potato
½ cup chopped onion
½ cup chopped celery
¼ teaspoon salt
1 cup water
1 (10¾-ounce) can condensed
   Manhattan-style clam
   chowder, undiluted

1 cup milk
1 (7½-ounce) can minced
   clams, drained
3 tablespoons dry white wine
½ cup whipping cream,
   whipped
Salt and pepper to taste
2 tablespoons snipped parsley

Combine first five ingredients in large saucepan. Cover, and cook until potato is tender, about 10 minutes; mash slightly. Add chowder, milk, clams, and wine. Heat but do not boil. Stir whipped cream into chowder. Season with salt and pepper; sprinkle with parsley. Yield: 4 servings.

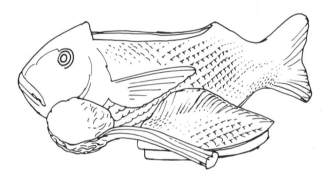

FAVORITE CLAM CHOWDER

18 large clams
½ cup butter
2 stalks celery, chopped
2 medium onions, chopped
2 carrots, sliced
1 green pepper, chopped
1 clove garlic, minced

1 teaspoon paprika
Bouquet garni
½ cup tomato puree
3 medium potatoes, cubed
½ teaspoon salt
½ teaspoon white pepper
1 cup plum tomatoes, chopped

Scrub clams and boil in enough water to cover. Remove clams from shell, finely chop, and reserve. Strain liquid and add enough water to make 8 cups; reserve.

Melt butter; add celery, onions, carrots, and green pepper. Cook until onions are tender. Add garlic and paprika and sauté briefly.

Add reserved stock and bouquet garni (which contains ¼ teaspoon each of thyme, rosemary, and pickling spices tied in cheesecloth).

Add tomato puree, clams, potatoes, salt, and pepper. Allow to simmer until potatoes and carrots are tender. Add tomatoes; cook for 10 minutes. Adjust seasonings. Remove bouquet garni. Yield: 8 servings.

LONG ISLAND CLAM CHOWDER

2 large onions, chopped
1 clove garlic, minced
4 medium carrots, pared and
   diced
1 cup diced celery
1 green pepper, diced
1 medium potato, pared and
   cubed
1 bay leaf
2 teaspoons salt
½ teaspoon monosodium
   glutamate

¼ teaspoon pepper
3 quarts water
1 (16-ounce) can whole
   tomatoes
1 tablespoon thyme
½ teaspoon rosemary
3 dozen large clams in liquor
3 tablespoons cubed salt pork
½ cup all-purpose flour
1 tablespoon chopped parsley

Combine onions, garlic, carrots, celery, green pepper, potato, bay leaf, salt, monosodium glutamate, pepper, and water in a large kettle; cook slowly about 30 minutes or until vegetables are tender. Add tomatoes, thyme, and rosemary; simmer 5 minutes. Drain clams, reserve liquor; remove and discard dark portions; cut clams into small pieces. Cook salt pork in small saucepan until brown and crisp; remove pork bits; reserve. Blend flour into drippings; add clam liquor; pour into chowder; simmer, stirring constantly, until thickened. Add clams, parsley, and pork bits; simmer 5 minutes longer. Remove bay leaf. Yield: 6 to 8 servings.

MANHATTAN CLAM CHOWDER

3 slices bacon, diced
1 cup chopped onion
1 cup chopped celery
½ green pepper, diced
1 (28-ounce) can whole
   tomatoes
3 (7½-ounce) cans minced
   clams, undrained
3 cups fish stock or water
   (See Index)

1 teaspoon salt
¼ teaspoon freshly ground
   black pepper
1 bay leaf
½ teaspoon thyme
3 cups diced potatoes
2 tablespoons minced parsley
2 tablespoons butter or
   margarine

Fry bacon until almost crisp in large Dutch oven or heavy kettle. Add onion, celery, and green pepper; cook slowly about 10 minutes, stirring occasionally, until vegetables are tender and golden. Stir in tomatoes.

Drain clams, reserving liquid; set clams aside. Add clam liquid to soup pot along with fish stock or water. Add salt, pepper, bay leaf, and thyme. Bring to boiling point, reduce heat to a simmer, cover, and cook slowly about 1 hour. Add potatoes; continue cooking about 30 minutes or until potatoes are quite tender. Add reserved clams and cook uncovered for 15 minutes. Before serving remove bay leaf and stir in parsley and butter. Yield: about 12 servings.

OCRACOKE CLAM CHOWDER

1 (1-inch-thick) slice salt pork
2½ pounds potatoes, peeled
    and diced
1½ pints fresh minced clams

1 onion, chopped
3 quarts water
2¼ teaspoons salt

Fry salt pork over medium heat in a large Dutch oven until done. Remove pork, reserving drippings in pan.

Dice pork; combine with potatoes, clams, onion, water, and salt in Dutch oven. Bring to a boil, and reduce heat; cover and simmer 2 hours and 15 minutes or until potatoes are tender. Yield: 8 to 12 servings.

HALIBUT CHOWDER

1 pound halibut, cut up
4 large tomatoes, peeled and
    quartered
4 large potatoes, peeled and
    diced
2 large onions, sliced

1 quart water
2 teaspoons salt
½ teaspoon pepper
⅔ cup butter or margarine
1 cup whipping cream
Thin tomato slices

Combine halibut, tomatoes, potatoes, onions, water, salt, and pepper in large saucepan. Bring to boil; reduce heat. Cover; simmer for 1 hour. Add butter and whipping cream; simmer for 5 minutes longer. Serve in large soup bowls. Garnish with tomato slices. Yield: 8 to 10 servings.

OYSTER CHOWDER

1 long thin slice salt pork,
    diced (about ½ cup)
1 large onion, diced
1 cup hot water
1 large potato, diced
1 teaspoon salt

1 pint oysters, quartered
2 cups half-and-half
Additional salt and black
    pepper to taste
Cayenne pepper to taste

Fry salt pork until lightly browned in a large, heavy pan. Add onion and sauté for about 5 minutes until soft but not browned. Drain off drippings, leaving salt pork and onion in pan. Add water, potato, and salt; cover pan and cook for about 7 minutes until potato is tender. Reduce heat to low; add oysters, and cook for about 5 minutes or until the edges curl. Heat half-and-half to scalding point in top of a double boiler; stir into oyster mixture. Remove from heat; add salt, black pepper, and cayenne pepper. Serve immediately. Yield: 4 to 6 servings.

SALMON CHOWDER

1 (16-ounce) can salmon	1 teaspoon salt
1 quart milk	Pepper to taste
¼ cup margarine	½ cup cracker crumbs

Drain salmon; remove bone and flake. Scald milk in top of double boiler; add margarine, salt, pepper, salmon, and cracker crumbs. Serve in warm bowls. Yield: 4 to 6 servings.

SALMON-CORN CHOWDER

1 (16-ounce) can salmon	¼ teaspoon freshly ground
1 quart water	white pepper
1 (12-ounce) can whole	1½ teaspoons salt
kernel corn	1 bay leaf, broken in two
1 (11-ounce) can tomato	4 dashes of hot sauce
bisque, undiluted	¼ cup finely chopped celery
¼ teaspoon lemon bits or	leaves
grated lemon rind	1 cup half-and-half or milk
¼ teaspoon Ac'cent	

Combine all ingredients except half-and-half in a large soup kettle or saucepan; blend thoroughly. Bring to boil over medium heat; cover and simmer for 40 minutes, stirring occasionally. Add half-and-half slowly and cook 15 minutes longer keeping kettle covered. Yield: 6 servings.

SEAFOOD CHOWDER

½ cup diced salt pork	2 cups diced potato
1 tablespoon butter	½ teaspoon sage
1 medium onion, diced	½ teaspoon pepper
2 tablespoons all-purpose flour	1 teaspoon thyme
2 cups boiling water	Salt to taste
1½ cups tomato juice	1 cup crabmeat
1 (12-ounce) can clam juice	½ cup peeled raw shrimp
1 cup diced celery	1 (12-ounce) jar small oysters
½ cup chopped green pepper	

Scald pork by covering with hot water for a few minutes; drain. Heat pork with butter in a large pan; add onion and cook over medium heat until browned. Blend in flour; gradually stir in water, tomato juice, and clam juice. Add celery, green pepper, potato, and seasonings. Simmer about 30 minutes or until vegetables are tender. Add crabmeat and shrimp; simmer 10 additional minutes. Add oysters and cook for 5 minutes or until edges curl. Yield: 6 servings.

SHRIMP CHOWDER

3 (4½- or 5-ounce) cans
   shrimp
¼ cup chopped onion
2 tablespoons salad oil
1 cup boiling water

1 cup diced potato
½ teaspoon salt
Dash of pepper
2 cups milk
Chopped parsley

Drain shrimp and rinse with cold water; cut large shrimp in half. Sauté onion in oil until tender. Add boiling water, potato, and seasonings. Cover and cook for 15 minutes or until potato is tender. Add milk and shrimp; heat. Garnish with parsley. Yield: 6 servings.

PACIFIC CHOWDER

4 slices bacon
¼ cup chopped onion
2 tablespoons chopped green
   pepper
1 (10¾-ounce) can condensed
   cream of potato soup,
   undiluted

2 cups milk
1 (6½- to 7-ounce) can tuna
   fish, drained
Dash of paprika

Cook bacon until crisp; drain, reserving 2 tablespoons drippings. In reserved drippings, cook onion and green pepper until tender but not brown. Add soup and milk; heat just to boiling. Break tuna fish into chunks and crumble bacon; add to soup. Heat. Top each serving with paprika. Yield: 4 servings.

TUNA CHOWDER

1 teaspoon salt
1½ tablespoons all-purpose
   flour
3 dashes of hot sauce
3 tablespoons water

5 cups milk
2 tablespoons butter
2 (6½-ounce) cans chunk
   light tuna fish

Combine salt, flour, hot sauce, and water in a large saucepan. Gradually stir in milk and butter. Drain all oil from 1 can of tuna fish. Add both cans tuna fish to milk mixture. Heat over medium heat, stirring frequently, until hot. Turn off heat, cover pan, and let pan remain on burner for 10 minutes. Yield: 4 to 5 servings.

• *Do not thaw fish at room temperature or in warm water; it will lose moisture and flavor. Instead place in refrigerator to thaw; allow 18 to 24 hours for thawing a 1-pound package. Do not refreeze thawed fish.*
• *Fish and onion odors can be removed from the hands by rubbing them with a little vinegar, followed by washing in soapy water.*

LIMA BEAN-HAM CHOWDER

1½ cups large dried lima
  beans
1 quart water
1 (1-pound) meaty ham hock
1 teaspoon salt
1 cup chopped onion
½ cup chopped green pepper

2 tablespoons melted butter or
  margarine
1 (8¾-ounce) can cream-style
  corn
2 cups milk
Salt and pepper to taste

Combine beans and water; bring to a boil, and simmer 2 minutes. Remove
from heat, and let stand 1 hour. Add ham hock; cover and simmer 1 hour
or until meat is tender. Add 1 teaspoon salt, and simmer 30 minutes.

Remove ham hock, and slightly mash beans with potato masher. Remove meat from ham hock; shred.

Sauté onion and green pepper in butter until tender; add to limas along
with ham, corn, and milk; heat thoroughly, but do not boil. Season to taste
with salt and pepper. Yield: 4 to 6 servings.

BEAN CHOWDER

¾ cup dried beans
3 cups water
1½ teaspoons salt
¾ cup diced potato
1 small onion, chopped
1½ teaspoons all-purpose
  flour

¾ cup cooked or canned
  whole tomatoes
⅓ cup shredded green pepper
1 to 2 tablespoons butter or
  margarine
1½ cups milk

Soak beans in water for 4 hours; add salt, and cook until almost done. Add potato and onion; cook 30 minutes. With the longer-cooking beans more water may be needed.

Combine flour and a little of the tomato; add to beans and stir. Add remaining tomato, green pepper, and butter. Cook for 10 minutes, stirring occasionally to prevent sticking. Stir in milk and reheat quickly. Yield: 4 servings.

BROCCOLI CHOWDER

2 pounds fresh broccoli
2 (13¾-ounce) cans chicken
  broth, undiluted
3 cups milk
1 cup chopped cooked ham
2 teaspoons salt

¼ teaspoon pepper
1 cup half-and-half
2 cups (½ pound) shredded
  Swiss cheese
¼ cup butter or margarine

Combine broccoli and 1 can chicken broth in a Dutch oven; cover and cook 7 minutes or until broccoli is crisp-tender. Remove broccoli from broth; cook, and chop coarsely.

Add remaining can of chicken broth, milk, ham, salt, and pepper to Dutch oven; bring to a boil over medium heat, stirring occasionally. Stir in broccoli and remaining ingredients. Cook over low heat until thoroughly heated (do not boil). Yield: 6 to 8 servings.

QUICK GREEN BEAN AND CORN CHOWDER

1 large onion, diced
1 large carrot, diced
¼ teaspoon thyme
2 tablespoons bacon drippings
1 quart water
⅔ cup grated, peeled potato

2 cups canned or cooked cut
  green beans
1 cup cream-style corn
2 cups milk
Salt and pepper to taste

Sauté onion, carrot, and thyme in bacon drippings in kettle for 7 minutes. Do not let vegetables brown. Add water and potato. Cover and cook 20 minutes. Add beans, corn, milk, salt, and pepper. Heat thoroughly. Yield: 4 servings.

CORN CHOWDER

½ pound bacon, cut into
   1-inch pieces
2 small onions, peeled and
   sliced
1 tablespoon all-purpose flour
1 cup water
2 cups finely diced potato

½ cup chopped celery
2 bay leaves
2 (17-ounce) cans cream-style
   corn
1 cup milk
1 teaspoon salt
¼ teaspoon white pepper

Fry bacon until crisp, and drain on paper towel; reserve ¼ cup bacon drippings and place in kettle. Sauté onions in bacon drippings for 5 minutes. Blend in flour and mix to a smooth paste. Gradually add water and stir until smooth. Add potato, celery, and bay leaves. Cover and cook over low heat about 15 minutes or until potato is done. Stir occasionally. Blend in corn, milk, seasonings, and bacon. Heat for 15 minutes. Remove bay leaves and serve hot. Yield: 5 to 6 servings.

PRAIRIE CORN CHOWDER

3 tablespoons diced salt pork
   or bacon
1 medium onion, chopped
2 cups cubed potato
2 cups boiling water
2 (17-ounce) cans cream-style
   corn
1 quart milk

2 teaspoons salt
¼ teaspoon pepper
¼ teaspoon rosemary
¼ cup diced pimiento
¼ cup shredded Cheddar
   cheese
2 tablespoons minced parsley

Brown salt pork in large heavy kettle; remove browned bits and reserve. Add onion and sauté until soft, but not browned. Add potato and water; simmer about 20 minutes or until potato is cooked. Add corn, milk, salt, pepper, rosemary, pimiento, and browned pork bits; heat until steaming hot. Add cheese and parsley. Yield: 4 to 6 servings.

VEGETABLE CHOWDER

2 cups diced carrots
3 cups diced potatos
1 cup diced celery
1 cup diced onion
12 slices bacon, cooked and
   crumbled
1 (8¾-ounce) can whole
   kernel corn, undrained

1 (10¾-ounce) condensed
   tomato soup, undiluted
1 cup half-and-half
1 cup milk
1 teaspoon salt
½ teaspoon pepper

Combine carrots, potatoes, celery, and onion; cook in water to cover until tender. Drain. Combine cooked vegetables and remaining ingredients. Simmer until well heated. Yield: 8 to 10 servings.

OKRA CHOWDER

1 small onion, finely chopped
1½ tablespoons melted butter
   or margarine
1 medium tomato, peeled and
   chopped
⅛ teaspoon thyme
1 bay leaf

1 tablespoon chopped parsley
1 quart water
1 (2½-ounce) envelope tomato
   vegetable soup mix with
   noodles
1 (10-ounce) package frozen
   okra, thinly sliced

Sauté onion in butter in medium size saucepan pan until tender. Add tomato, thyme, bay leaf, and parsley. Cover and cook for 5 minutes. Add water and soup mix. Bring to a boil, stirring occasionally. Add okra and simmer for 15 minutes. Remove bay leaf. Yield: 6 servings.

SPINACH CHOWDER

2 cups chopped spinach
1 cup water
3 medium potatoes, sliced
3 slices bacon

½ cup sliced onion
3 tablespoons all-purpose flour
1 cup evaporated milk
2 teaspoons salt

Add spinach to 1 cup boiling water. Cover; lower heat, and simmer 3 to 5 minutes. Drain, reserving liquid.

Cook potatoes in salted water to cover until tender. Drain, reserving liquid.

Fry bacon in a Dutch oven until brown; remove bacon, and reserve drippings. Drain bacon thoroughly on a paper towel; crumble, and set aside.

Sauté onion in bacon drippings until lightly browned. Blend in flour; gradually add milk, spinach liquid, and potato water. Cook, stirring constantly, until mixture boils and thickens. Add salt, spinach, and potatoes. Bring to a boil; lower heat, and simmer 5 minutes. Garnish each serving with crumbled bacon. Yield: 6 to 8 servings.

TOMATO CHOWDER

1 cup sliced onion
¾ cup chopped celery
3 tablespoons melted butter or
   margarine
1 (16-ounce) can cut green
   beans
1 (16-ounce) can whole
   kernel corn

1 (16-ounce) can whole
   tomatoes
2 cups diced potato
2 teaspoons salt
½ teaspoon Worcestershire
   sauce
1 (7-ounce) can tuna fish,
   drained and flaked

Sauté onion and celery in butter until tender. Drain green beans and corn; reserve liquid and add water to measure 5 cups. Add liquid to onion and celery with tomatoes, potato, salt, and Worcestershire sauce. Cook over low heat about 30 minutes. Add beans, corn, and flaked tuna fish. Heat to serving temperature. Yield: 12 servings.

creams
& purees

If soups are a favorite at your house, but you are tired of the same old standbys, try one of these cream soups. Interesting main ingredients such as almonds, avocados, and peanuts give them an unusual twist.

Cream soups are equally delicious hot or cold and are ideal for the appetizer course of an elegant dinner or as the main dish for a light lunch or supper. Complete the meal with a salad, a good bread, and a substantial dessert.

Cream soups are made smooth with cream or milk, broth, and pureed vegetables. Homemade broths are always extra tasty, although there are some excellent canned broths on the market. Just before serving, garnish soup with something interesting like dillweed, croutons, or chopped peanuts.

BLUE CHEESE AND RED CAVIAR SOUP

½ to ¾ cup crumbled blue
  cheese
¼ cup water
¼ teaspoon each of basil,
  chervil, oregano, and
  pepper

1 (8-ounce) carton commercial
  sour cream
½ to 1 cup milk
1 (4-ounce) jar red caviar

Blend cheese and water in blender for two seconds. Combine seasonings; add to mixture along with sour cream. Use milk to thin mixture according to taste. Cover and chill for 24 hours. Serve with a spoonful of caviar. Yield: 4 to 5 servings.

HELVETIA SOUP

1 cup chopped onion
⅓ cup melted butter or
  margarine
6 cups small dry bread cubes
1½ quarts chicken broth
2 egg yolks, beaten

1 cup half-and-half
1½ cups shredded Swiss
  cheese
Salt to taste
White pepper to taste
Grated nutmeg

Sauté onion in butter until tender; add bread cubes, stirring until well coated and lightly browned. Stir in chicken broth, and simmer over low heat 8 minutes. Cool slightly.

Pour broth mixture in container of electric blender; puree. Pour into saucepan; add egg yolks, half-and-half, and cheese, mixing well. Season with salt, pepper, and nutmeg. Heat thoroughly. Yield: 8 to 10 servings.

CREAM OF ALMOND SOUP

½ cup almonds
1 tablespoon water
1 cup milk
1 cup half-and-half
Rind of 1 lemon, cut in 1 thin
  strip
¼ cup butter or margarine

¼ cup all-purpose flour
1 quart beef broth
⅛ teaspoon salt
⅛ teaspoon pepper
Dash of cayenne pepper
½ teaspoon ground mace

Grind almonds; pound to a paste, adding water to prevent oiliness. Scald milk and half-and-half with lemon rind in a medium saucepan; set aside.

Melt butter in a large saucepan; stir in flour, blending well. Gradually stir in broth; cook 5 to 10 minutes, stirring constantly, until smooth and thickened. Add scalded milk mixture, seasonings, and almond paste. Cook over medium heat 15 minutes. Remove lemon rind before serving. Yield: 6 servings.

MANDELMILCHSUPPE

2 cups ground blanched
  almonds
½ cup melted butter
2 quarts milk
6 chicken bouillon cubes

4 teaspoons cornstarch
½ teaspoon sugar
2 teaspoons monosodium
  glutamate
Toasted, slivered almonds

Sauté ground almonds in butter until lightly browned; stir in milk. Crush bouillon cubes and mix with cornstarch, sugar, and monosodium glutamate; stir into almond mixture. Simmer, stirring frequently, until slightly thickened. Serve in soup bowls, and garnish with toasted, slivered almonds. Yield: 8 to 10 servings.

PEANUT SOUP

1 medium onion, minced
1 cup sliced celery
½ cup butter or margarine
2 tablespoons all-purpose flour
2 quarts chicken broth

1 cup creamy peanut butter
1 cup half-and-half
¼ cup chopped parsley
¼ cup chopped salted peanuts

Sauté onion and celery in butter until tender. Stir in flour, blending well. Stir in chicken broth; cook, stirring frequently, until mixture comes to a boil. Reduce heat to simmer; stir in peanut butter and half-and-half. Simmer 5 to 10 minutes. Top with parsley and peanuts before serving. Yield: about 10 servings.

CREAM OF JERUSALEM ARTICHOKE SOUP

1 large onion, diced
2 tablespoons butter or
  margarine, divided
2 cups peeled, cubed
  Jerusalem artichokes
1 tablespoon all-purpose flour

½ teaspoon salt
⅛ teaspoon ground nutmeg
Pinch of sugar
2 cups water
1 cup evaporated milk
1 egg yolk, slightly beaten

Sauté onion in 1 tablespoon butter 5 minutes in a Dutch oven; add artichoke, and sauté 3 minutes. Stir in flour, salt, nutmeg, and sugar; gradually add water, stirring constantly. Cook over medium heat until artichoke is tender.

Mash artichoke in liquid; add milk, and simmer 5 to 10 minutes. Add 1 tablespoon butter. Stir a small amount of hot mixture into egg yolk; gradually add to remaining hot mixture, stirring well. Yield: 6 to 8 servings.

ASPARAGUS SOUP

1 (2-ounce) envelope noodle
soup mix with real chicken
broth
1½ cups boiling water
1 tablespoon butter or
margarine

1 (10-ounce) package frozen
asparagus spears, cooked
and drained
2 cups milk

Combine soup mix, water, butter, and asparagus in blender; blend 2 minutes or until smooth. Heat milk in medium saucepan; stir in asparagus mixture. Cook 2 to 3 minutes, stirring occasionally. Serve hot or cold. Yield: 4 servings.

CREAMY ASPARAGUS SOUP

1 (10-ounce) package frozen
cut asparagus
½ cup boiling chicken broth
(See Index)
2 egg yolks
1¼ cups milk

½ teaspoon salt
¼ teaspoon white pepper
2 drops hot sauce
Chopped parsley
Paprika

Combine asparagus and chicken broth; cook, uncovered, for 8 minutes after it returns to a boil. Put asparagus and broth into blender and blend until smooth; add egg yolks and blend. Return to pan and stir in milk, salt, pepper, and hot sauce. Reheat just before serving, but do not boil. Top each serving with parsley and paprika. Yield: 4 to 6 servings.

FROSTED ASPARAGUS SOUP

1 (9-ounce) package frozen
asparagus tips
1 (8-ounce) carton commercial
sour cream, divided
1 (2¾-ounce) package leek
soup mix

2½ cups milk
1 teaspoon lemon juice
Chopped chives

Cook asparagus according to package directions; drain. Combine asparagus, ¾ cup sour cream, soup mix, milk, and lemon juice in blender container; process until smooth. Chill thoroughly. Garnish with remaining sour cream, and sprinkle with chives. Yield: 4 to 5 servings.

AVOCADO SOUP

2 large avocados, peeled and
diced
2 cups half-and-half
2 cups chicken broth (See
Index)

2 cups clam juice
¼ cup sherry
Avocado slices (optional)

Place avocados and half-and-half in blender; blend until smooth. Heat broth and clam juice in saucepan; add avocado-cream mixture and sherry. Heat, stirring constantly. Serve hot or chilled. Garnish with additional slices of avocado, if desired. Yield: 4 to 6 servings.

AVOCADO-CLAM SOUP

2 large avocados, diced	2 cups chicken broth (See
2 cups half-and-half	Index)
1 (10¾-ounce) can condensed	Salt and pepper to taste
New England style clam	¼ cup sherry
chowder, undiluted	

Place avocados, half-and-half, and clam chowder in blender; blend until smooth. Heat broth, and add avocado mixture and seasonings; heat to serving temperature. Add sherry just before serving. Yield: 5 to 6 servings.

CHILLED AVOCADO SOUP

3 ripe avocados, peeled and	¼ teaspoon onion salt
coarsely chopped	Pinch of white pepper
1 cup chicken broth	1 teaspoon lemon juice
1 cup half-and-half	Lemon slices
1 teaspoon salt	

Combine avocado and chicken broth in container of electric blender. Cover and blend until smooth. Remove from blender container, and stir in half-and-half, salt, onion salt, and white pepper. Cover and refrigerate overnight.

Before serving, stir in lemon juice. Garnish with lemon slices. Yield: 4 to 6 servings.

Photograph for this recipe on page 40

CREAM OF AVOCADO SOUP

1 large avocado, peeled and	⅛ teaspoon hot pepper flakes
sliced	or hot sauce
1½ cups chicken broth (See	1½ cups crushed ice
Index)	½ cup half-and-half
1 clove garlic	Chopped chives or parsley

Put avocado, chicken broth, garlic, and pepper flakes into blender. Cover and blend on high speed for 15 seconds. Add ice and half-and-half; cover and blend for 10 seconds longer. If too thick, thin with more broth or half-and-half; serve sprinkled with chives or parsley. Yield: 6 servings.

MAHOGANY VELVET SOUP

1 (11-ounce) can condensed
   black bean soup, undiluted
1 (10½-ounce) can condensed
   consommé, undiluted

1¼ cups water
1 tablespoon sherry
Lemon slices

Place black bean soup in blender; add consommé and water, and blend until smooth. Heat thoroughly in saucepan. Add sherry just before removing from heat. Serve hot or chilled. Garnish with lemon slices. Yield: 4 servings.

CREAM OF BROCCOLI SOUP

2 (10-ounce) packages frozen
   chopped broccoli
1 stalk celery, sliced
1 onion, sliced
1 bay leaf
4 whole black peppercorns

1 cup boiling water
2 teaspoons salt
2 cups milk
⅛ teaspoon pepper
⅛ teaspoon ground nutmeg

Cook broccoli, celery, onion, bay leaf, and peppercorns in boiling salted water in a covered saucepan for about 30 minutes or until very tender. Discard bay leaf and peppercorns.

Blend broccoli mixture in blender, a small amount at a time, or press through sieve. Combine broccoli puree, milk, pepper, and nutmeg in saucepan. Heat slowly, stirring, until heated thoroughly. Yield: 6 to 8 servings.

CREAMY BROCCOLI SOUP

1 (10-ounce) package frozen
   broccoli
2 tablespoons minced onion
2 beef bouillon cubes

½ cup boiling water
2 cups half-and-half
Salt and pepper to taste

Cook broccoli, adding onion, according to directions on package; drain. Dissolve beef bouillon cubes in boiling water, and add to broccoli. Place in blender and blend until smooth. Remove from blender; add half-and-half and seasonings, and heat to serving temperature. Yield: 6 servings.

CREAM OF CARROT SOUP

¼ cup butter or margarine
1 potato, peeled and thinly
  sliced
2 onions, thinly sliced
7 large carrots, thinly sliced
1 clove garlic, chopped
Salt and pepper

½ cup water
1 tablespoon all-purpose flour
3 cups milk
⅛ teaspoon savory
Chopped chives
Chopped parsley

Melt butter in a saucepan; add vegetables, garlic, salt, pepper, and water. Cover and cook until vegetables are very tender when pierced with a fork.

Stir in flour, milk, and savory. Bring soup to a boil, reduce heat, and let simmer for 20 minutes. Put soup through a fine sieve or blend in blender; add chives and parsley. Chill. Yield: 4 servings.

CAULIFLOWER CREAM SOUP

1 (¾-pound) head of
  cauliflower
4 medium potatoes, peeled
  and diced
6 cups scalded milk, divided

½ teaspoon salt
2 tablespoons butter
4 slices French bread
Butter
Finely chopped parsley

Cook cauliflower in lightly salted water for 5 minutes. Drain. Combine cauliflower, potatoes, 4 cups scalded milk, and salt. Bring to a boil, cover pan, and simmer for 30 minutes. Strain, reserving liquid. Mash vegetables; stir into reserved liquid. Add remaining scalded milk and bring to a boil. Remove from heat; stir in 2 tablespoons butter.

Cut French bread into cubes and brown in butter. Place bread cubes in bottom of soup bowls; pour soup over cubes. Add a dash chopped parsley and serve hot. Yield: 4 servings.

CELERY CREAM SOUP

2 cups chopped celery
1 large onion, chopped
½ bay leaf
1 clove garlic, minced
2 cups water
2 tablespoons margarine
¼ cup all-purpose flour

1 cup instant nonfat dry milk
  solids
½ teaspoon salt
Dash of pepper
½ teaspoon Worcestershire
  sauce

Combine celery, onion, bay leaf, garlic, and water; cook about 15 minutes or until celery is tender. Remove bay leaf; drain, reserving liquid. Set vegetables aside. Add enough water to reserved liquid to make 2 cups.

Melt margarine in a heavy saucepan; stir in flour and dry milk. Slowly add reserved liquid to flour mixture, stirring constantly, until smooth and thickened. Add salt, pepper, and Worcestershire sauce, stirring well.

Combine vegetables and cream sauce; process in blender until smooth. Remove from blender; heat to serving temperature. Yield: 4 servings.

CELERY-CUCUMBER SOUP

1 (10½-ounce) can cream of
   celery soup, undiluted
1 cup milk
¼ cup cottage cheese
¼ cup coarsely chopped
   cucumber

2 tablespoons coarsely
   chopped green pepper
1 teaspoon coarsely chopped
   onion

Combine all ingredients in container of electric blender; process until smooth. Chill. Yield: 3 to 4 servings.

COLD CREAM OF CUCUMBER SOUP

1 medium onion, chopped
5 cucumbers, peeled, seeded,
   and chopped
½ cup melted butter
½ cup all-purpose flour
1½ quarts hot beef or chicken
   broth (See Index)

2 cups hot milk
1 cup half-and-half
Salt
White pepper
Chopped chives

Sauté onion and cucumber in butter. When ingredients are soft, add flour to form a roux. Add hot broth and let simmer 15 minutes. Then add hot milk and let simmer 10 minutes longer. Remove from heat and pour through sieve. Add half-and-half and season with salt and pepper. Chill. Add some chives to each cup of soup, and serve in crushed ice. Yield: 8 servings.

COOL CUCUMBER SOUP

3 small cucumbers
1 bunch (about 1 cup)
   scallions, chopped
3 cups water, divided
2 teaspoons salt
Dash of cayenne pepper
3 tablespoons all-purpose flour

2 cups water, divided
1 tablespoon finely snipped
   fresh mint
1 cup whipping cream
Green food color
Mint sprigs

Peel 2 cucumbers; thinly slice all 3 cucumbers to make about 3 cups. Combine cucumbers, scallions, 1 cup water, salt, and cayenne pepper in saucepan. Bring to a boil; reduce heat and simmer, covered, about 30 minutes or until vegetables are mushy.

Make paste of flour and ½ cup water; stir paste into cucumber mixture. Add 1½ cups water. Bring to a boil, stirring; simmer about 5 minutes or until thickened.

Blend cucumber mixture, a small amount at a time in blender, or press through sieve to make a smooth mixture. Stir in mint, cream, and enough green food color to make a light green. Cover, and refrigerate.

Serve in well-chilled goblets or glasses. Garnish with mint sprigs. Yield: 8 servings.

FRESH LETTUCE BISQUE

2 tablespoons butter or
    margarine
½ cup chopped scallions
¼ cup chopped parsley
1 (10½-ounce) can condensed
    beef broth, undiluted
1 cup water

7 cups (1 head) torn iceberg
    lettuce leaves
1 cup half-and-half
1 teaspoon salt
⅛ teaspoon pepper
½ teaspoon tarragon

Melt butter in a large saucepan; add scallions and parsley. Cook over
medium heat until scallions are tender. Stir in beef broth, water, and
lettuce leaves. Cover and simmer 25 minutes.

Puree in blender or food mill. Return to saucepan; stir in remaining
ingredients. Serve hot or cold. Yield: 6 to 8 servings.

CREAM OF GREEN ONION SOUP

2 cups water
4 teaspoons chicken-seasoned
    stock base
½ teaspoon monosodium
    glutamate

15 green onions and tops,
    chopped
½ cup commercial sour cream
1 teaspoon chopped green
    onion

Place water, stock base, monosodium glutamate, and green onions in a
2-quart saucepan. Cook over medium heat for approximately 8 minutes.
Place in blender and blend for 30 seconds. Place in individual soup bowls
and add a large dollop of sour cream to each bowl. Garnish with chopped
green onion. Yield: 6 servings.

ONION AND CELERY CREAM SOUP

1½ cups minced onion
½ cup minced celery
1 cup hot chicken broth (See
    Index)
½ teaspoon salt
3 tablespoons butter
3 tablespoons all-purpose flour
2 cups hot milk

1 teaspoon salt
¼ teaspoon freshly ground
    black pepper
⅛ teaspoon ground nutmeg
½ cup whipping cream,
    heated
1 to 2 tablespoons chopped
    pistachio nuts (optional)

Combine onion, celery, broth, and ½ teaspoon salt; simmer, covered,
until onion and celery are very soft. Rub through a sieve, put through a
food mill, or puree in blender. Heat butter in a saucepan and stir in flour.
Gradually blend in milk. Cook over medium heat, stirring constantly, until
smooth and thickened. Add remaining salt, pepper, nutmeg, and pureed
vegetables. Cook until heated thoroughly. Stir in cream. Sprinkle with
chopped pistachio nuts, if desired. Yield: 4 servings.

CLOVER GREEN SOUP

1 (10¾-ounce) can condensed
   cream of celery soup,
   undiluted
1 (11½-ounce) can condensed
   green pea soup, undiluted

1 soup can water
1 soup can milk

Combine soups in saucepan and stir until smooth. Gradually blend in water and milk. Heat, stirring occasionally. Serve hot. Yield: 4 to 6 servings.

CREAM OF GREEN PEPPER SOUP

1 medium-size green pepper,
   chopped
½ small onion, chopped
2 tablespoons melted butter or
   margarine

1 (10¾-ounce) can condensed
   cream of celery soup,
   undiluted
1 soup can of milk

Sauté pepper and onion in butter for 5 minutes. Place pepper mixture in blender and blend well. Add soup and milk. Blend a few seconds until smooth. Heat soup gently. Yield: 3 servings.

PIMIENTO CREAM SOUP

¼ cup butter
¼ cup all-purpose flour
2 cups milk
2 cups half-and-half
1 quart chicken stock

2 (4-ounce) cans pimiento
1 teaspoon grated onion
Salt and pepper to taste
Dash of cayenne pepper

In a 3-quart heavy saucepan, melt butter, and blend in the flour to make a roux. Slowly add milk, stirring briskly so no lumps will form, and cook until thickened. Gradually add half-and-half and stock. Sieve pimientos or whirl in blender to puree. Add to soup along with onion, salt, pepper, and cayenne. Cook over lowest heat, not boiling, 10 minutes. Yield: 8 to 10 servings.

EASY VICHYSSOISE

3 cups peeled sliced potatoes
3 cups sliced white of leek
1½ quarts chicken broth (See
   Index)

1 cup whipping cream
2 teaspoons salt
⅛ teaspoon white pepper
Chopped chives (optional)

Simmer potatoes and leek in chicken broth until potatoes are tender. Puree mixture in blender. Add cream, salt, and pepper; chill. Garnish with chives, if desired. Yield: 6 to 8 servings.

CRÈME VICHYSSOISE

4 leeks or 1½ cups minced
   onion
3 cups peeled and sliced
   potatoes
3 cups boiling water
4 chicken bouillon cubes
3 tablespoons butter or
   margarine

1 cup half-and-half or
   whipping cream
1 cup milk
1 teaspoon salt
¼ teaspoon pepper
2 tablespoons minced chives
¼ teaspoon paprika

Cut leeks and 3 inches of their green tops into fine pieces; cook with potatoes, covered, in boiling water about 40 minutes or until tender. Press, without draining, through fine sieve into double boiler. Add bouillon cubes and next 5 ingredients. Mix well; reheat. Chill. Serve very cold; top with chives and paprika. Yield: 6 servings.

CREAM OF PUMPKIN SOUP

½ cup sliced green onion
3 tablespoons melted butter or
   margarine
2 cups cooked mashed
   pumpkin
1 (10¾-ounce) can chicken
   broth

1 small tomato, peeled and
   chopped
½ teaspoon salt
Dash of pepper
1 cup half-and-half

Sauté onion in butter until tender; add remaining ingredients except half-and-half. Cover and simmer 10 minutes, stirring occasionally. Place mixture in blender container, and process until smooth. Add half-and-half, and heat through. Serve warm. Yield: 6 to 8 small servings.

SPICY PUMPKIN SOUP

1 (16-ounce) can mashed
   pumpkin
½ cup sugar
½ teaspoon salt
1 teaspoon ground cinnamon
½ teaspoon ground ginger

¼ teaspoon ground cloves
1⅔ cups evaporated or plain
   milk
2 tablespoons butter or
   margarine

Combine all ingredients except butter in top of double boiler. Heat until piping hot over boiling water. Stir in butter just before serving. Add more milk, if desired. Evaporated and plain milk may be combined. Yield: 4 servings.

COLD CREAM OF SPINACH SOUP

1 (10-ounce) package frozen chopped spinach	¼ cup all-purpose flour
2 teaspoons finely chopped onion	1 teaspoon salt
	⅛ teaspoon white pepper
2 tablespoons melted butter or margarine	1 quart milk, divided
	3 tablespoons lemon juice

Cook spinach according to package directions; drain well and set aside.

Sauté onion in butter; stir in flour, salt, and pepper. Cook over low heat, stirring constantly, until smooth and bubbly. Gradually stir in 2 cups milk; heat until mixture is thick.

Blend cream sauce and spinach; add remaining milk and lemon juice, and blend well. Cover and refrigerate at least 4 hours. Stir gently. Serve in chilled bowls or mugs. Yield: 6 to 8 servings.

Photograph for this recipe on page 147

CREAM OF SPINACH SOUP

2 cups chopped spinach	⅛ teaspoon pepper
¼ cup finely chopped onion	⅛ teaspoon mace
¼ cup finely chopped carrot	1 cup whipping cream, whipped
1 quart milk, divided	
2 teaspoons salt	

Combine spinach, onion, carrot, and 1 cup milk in top of double boiler. Cook, covered, until vegetables are tender. Press through a fine sieve. Add salt, pepper, and mace, and make a smooth paste. Add remaining 3 cups milk to the puree of vegetables. Simmer 10 minutes and, just before serving, fold in whipped cream. Pour into bowls. Yield: 6 servings.

SOUPE VERTE

1 (10-ounce) package frozen chopped spinach, thawed and drained	1 soup can milk
	2 tablespoons minced parsley
1 (10¾-ounce) can condensed cream of chicken soup, undiluted	

Puree spinach in blender. Heat soup and milk, stirring until smooth. Add spinach and parsley and cook 3 minutes longer. If soup is too thick, add a little cream or milk. Chill, if desired. Yield: 6 to 8 servings.

FROSTY TOMATO SOUP

1 (10¾-ounce) can condensed tomato soup, chilled and undiluted	Dash of hot pepper sauce
	Commercial sour cream
	Chopped chives or green onion tops
1 soup can chilled buttermilk	

Combine soup and buttermilk. Add pepper sauce, and pour into chilled soup bowls or cups. Top each with a spoonful of sour cream, and garnish with chopped chives or green onion tops. Serve at once. Yield: 4 servings.

CREAM OF TOMATO SOUP

2 tablespoons butter or margarine	1 tablespoon minced onion
3 tablespoons all-purpose flour	¼ teaspoon celery seeds
2 teaspoons salt, divided	½ teaspoon sugar
⅛ teaspoon pepper	½ bay leaf
2 cups milk	1 whole clove
1 (16-ounce) can whole tomatoes, undrained	Dash of soda

Melt butter in top of double boiler. Stir in flour, 1½ teaspoons salt, pepper, and milk. Cook, stirring constantly, until smooth and thickened.

Combine tomatoes, onion, celery seeds, ½ teaspoon salt, sugar, bay leaf, and whole clove in a saucepan. Simmer, uncovered, for 5 minutes. Remove bay leaf and whole clove; put remainder through food mill or blend in blender. Stir in soda. Just before serving, stir tomato mixture into milk mixture. Heat, stirring constantly. If soup curdles, beat with egg beater. Yield: 4 to 6 servings.

TOMATO YOGURT SOUP

2½ cups tomato juice	1 teaspoon salt
1¼ cups yogurt	¼ teaspoon pepper
¼ cup chopped celery	Chopped parsley or chives (optional)
1 tablespoon lemon juice	

Combine all ingredients except parsley in container of electric blender; process until smooth. Chill. Garnish with chopped parsley, if desired. Yield: 4 to 5 servings.

BLOODY MARY SOUP

4 to 5 ripe tomatoes	2 cups tomato juice
2 cloves garlic	Salt and pepper to taste
1 medium onion, sliced	½ cup vodka, chilled
1 small green pepper, cut into small pieces	4 celery sticks (optional)

Peel and seed tomatoes; place in blender container with garlic, onion, and green pepper. Blend to a smooth paste; gradually blend in tomato juice. Season. Chill thoroughly.

Just before serving, stir in vodka. Serve over ice in large goblets; use celery sticks for stirrers. Yield: 4 servings.

fruit soups

Perhaps the suggestion of a fruit soup may be new to you, but Europeans have long enjoyed sweet soups as a delicate appetizer or as a light ending to a special dinner.

So easy to prepare, these soups are made with fresh, dried, or frozen fruits. The consistency of fruit soups may be as thin as punch or as thick as pudding. The thinner and less sweet soups are flavored as appetizers; the thicker and sweeter soups are better for dessert.

Soups may be thinned with additional liquid or thickened with the addition of tapioca. Since fruit syrups may be substituted for water in these recipes, fruit soups provide a convenient way to use up canned fruit syrups.

Try one of these simple fruit soups and serve it in your prettiest glass bowls or champagne glasses. Garnish with fresh fruit, sour cream, or mint.

HONEY APPLE SOUP

6 cooking apples, pared,
    cored, and sliced
4¼ cups apple juice, divided
1 cup honey
2 tablespoons lemon juice

1 tablespoon quick-cooking
    tapioca
2 teaspoons grated lemon rind
Yogurt

Combine apple slices and 1 cup apple juice in a heavy saucepan; cover and cook until apples are soft, about 15 minutes.

Process apples in electric blender container until smooth, or press them through a sieve.

Return apple puree to saucepan; add honey, lemon juice, tapioca, and remaining apple juice. Cook over low heat until tapioca is soft and transparent and mixture is thickened. Chill thoroughly.

Serve soup very cold; garnish with lemon rind and yogurt. Yield: 6 to 8 servings.

CANTALOUPE SOUP

4 medium cantaloupes or
    honeydew melons
Light rum
2 tablespoons melted butter or
    margarine
¼ teaspoon ground nutmeg
1½ cups grapefruit juice

Juice of 2 limes
2 tablespoons honey
Salt and pepper to taste
¼ cup half-and-half
2 tablespoons orange-flavored
    liqueur

Using a melon ball scooper, scoop out 18 cantaloupe balls. Place in a small bowl, and cover with rum; chill at least 1 hour.

Dice enough remaining melon to yield 4 cups; sauté in butter 2 to 3 minutes, and sprinkle with nutmeg. Combine sautéed cantaloupe, grapefruit juice, lime juice, honey, salt, and pepper in container of electric blender; process until smooth. Stir in half-and-half and liqueur; chill thoroughly.

Just before serving, drain melon balls; place 3 in each serving dish, and add soup. Yield: 6 servings.

CHERRY SOUP

2 (16-ounce) cans pitted sour
    cherries, undrained
1½ tablespoons quick-cooking
    tapioca

1 cinnamon stick
½ cup sugar
Juice of 1 lemon
¼ teaspoon salt

Combine all ingredients in saucepan; cook over medium heat until thickened, stirring occasionally. Remove cinnamon stick. Serve chilled. Yield: 6 to 8 servings.

FRUIT SOUP

5 cups water
¼ cup quick-cooking tapioca
1 (8-ounce) can applesauce
1 cup apricot halves, pureed
½ cup golden raisins
1 cup sugar, divided
3 ripe bananas, well mashed
¾ cup orange juice
2 tablespoons lemon juice

2 tablespoons grated orange
    rind
¼ cup red maraschino
    cherries, drained and sliced
¼ cup green maraschino
    cherries, drained and sliced
Commercial sour cream
Orange and lemon slices

Combine water, tapioca, applesauce, apricots, raisins, and ½ cup sugar in large saucepan; heat until mixture becomes slightly thickened, stirring often. Combine ½ cup sugar and next 6 ingredients; add to tapioca mixture. Chill thoroughly. Serve in small bowls with a dollop of sour cream. Garnish with orange and lemon slices. Yield: 15 servings.

COLD FRUIT SOUP COCKTAIL

2 pears, peeled and quartered
2 peaches, peeled and sliced
1 cup grapes or cherries,
    halved and pitted
4 plums, pitted and cut into
    wedges

1 small lemon, thinly sliced
¾ cup water
¾ cup sugar
½ to ¾ cup gin
2 tablespoons lemon juice

Combine fruit in large bowl. Combine water and sugar in saucepan; bring to a boil and simmer for 5 minutes. Remove from heat; stir in gin and lemon juice. Pour over fruit; chill several hours. Yield: 4 servings.

Note: If frozen mixed fruits are substituted, thaw and add lemon juice, lemon slices, and gin.

GOLDEN FRUIT SOUP

1 cup dried prunes	1/8 teaspoon ground nutmeg
1/2 cup dried apricots	Dash of ground cloves
6 dried pear halves, cut into strips	1/8 teaspoon salt
1 quart apple cider	2 tablespoons light rum (optional)
2 tablespoons sugar	6 lemon slices
2 tablespoons lemon juice	6 whole cloves
1/8 teaspoon ground cinnamon	

Rinse and drain prunes, apricots, and pears. Combine fruit with cider in a saucepan; heat to boiling and simmer 20 to 30 minutes or until all the fruits are barely tender. Add sugar, lemon juice, spices, and salt. Add rum, if desired, just before serving. Serve hot or chilled. Garnish each serving with a lemon slice pierced with a whole clove. Yield: 6 servings.

FRUKTSOPPA

1 cup diced dried apricots	1 cup sugar
3/4 cup diced pitted prunes	1/4 cup quick-cooking tapioca
1 1/2 quarts water	2 tart red apples, peeled and diced
1 stick cinnamon	
1 orange, thinly sliced	1/2 cup seedless raisins
1 lemon, thinly sliced	1/4 cup dried currants

Combine apricots, prunes, and water in saucepan; let stand 30 minutes. Add cinnamon stick, orange, lemon, sugar, and tapioca; bring to a boil, cover, and simmer for 10 minutes.

Stir in apples, raisins, and currants; cook an additional 5 minutes or until apples are tender. Remove cinnamon stick. Chill thoroughly. Yield: 8 to 10 servings.

HOLIDAY SWEET SOUP

1 cup dried apricots	1/4 teaspoon ground nutmeg
1 cup dried prunes	Dash of ground cloves
1 quart apple cider	Dash of salt
2 tablespoons sugar	6 lemon slices
Juice of 1 lemon	6 whole cloves
1/4 teaspoon ground cinnamon	

Wash apricots and prunes; dry. Combine fruit with cider in a kettle and heat to boiling. Lower heat and simmer for 30 minutes or until fruit is tender. Add sugar, lemon juice, spices, and salt. Serve soup chilled or hot, and garnish each serving with a lemon slice pierced with a whole clove. Yield: 6 servings.

SCANDINAVIAN FRUIT SOUP

1 (6-ounce) package dried
   apricots, coarsely chopped
½ cup coarsely chopped
   prunes
1 cup seedless raisins
1 orange, sliced and seeded
1 lemon, sliced and seeded
3 to 4 tablespoons
   quick-cooking tapioca

1 cup sugar
1 stick cinnamon
3 cooking apples, pared,
   cored, and diced
1 (16-ounce) can pitted sour
   cherries, undrained

Combine apricots, prunes, raisins, orange and lemon slices, tapioca, sugar, and cinnamon; cover with water, and let stand overnight. In the morning, add 2 cups water and apples; cook over medium heat, stirring, until fruit is soft. Stir in cherries. Serve hot or cold. Yield: 6 to 8 servings.

SWEDISH FRUIT SOUP

1 (8-ounce) package mixed
   dried fruits, cut into
   bite-size pieces
2½ cups water
½ teaspoon ground cinnamon

1 (3-ounce) package
   cherry-flavored gelatin
3 cups orange juice
Commercial sour cream

Combine dried fruit, water, and cinnamon in a large saucepan; bring to a boil. Cover; reduce heat, and simmer 20 minutes.

Remove from heat, and stir in gelatin until dissolved; add orange juice. Chill.

Serve soup cold, topped with sour cream. Yield: about 8 servings.

BAYOU LEMON SOUP

3 (13¾-ounce) cans chicken broth or 1½ quarts homemade chicken broth	½ teaspoon white pepper
	1 teaspoon dried green onion
	⅓ cup strained lemon juice
2 tablespoons cold water	3 eggs
¼ cup uncooked regular rice	

In a saucepan bring chicken broth and water to a boil over high heat; add rice, pepper, and onion. Reduce heat to low and simmer about 15 minutes or until rice is tender. In a small bowl beat lemon juice and eggs until light and frothy. Pour small amount into hot broth, beating rapidly with a wire whisk; gradually add remaining egg mixture, beating constantly with whisk. Cook over low heat until broth reaches the boiling point. Remove at once; *do not allow to boil.* Serve hot. Yield: 6 servings.

CHILLED LEMON SOUP

3½ cups chicken broth	½ teaspoon salt
2 tablespoons quick-cooking tapioca	Dash of cayenne pepper
	1 cup whipping cream
2 eggs	Lemon slices (optional)
2 tablespoons lemon juice	
1 tablespoon grated lemon rind	

Bring broth to a boil; add tapioca, stirring to blend well. Reduce heat to low; cover and simmer 10 minutes.

Combine eggs, lemon juice, lemon rind, salt, and pepper; beat well, and stir in whipping cream. Stir ¼ cup hot broth into egg mixture; then gradually stir egg mixture into remaining broth. Cook over very low heat, stirring constantly, until mixture thickens and coats a metal spoon.

Remove soup from heat; cool. Chill thoroughly. Garnish with lemon slices, if desired. Yield: 6 to 8 servings.

LEMON MERINGUE SOUP

¼ cup cornstarch
1 quart water, divided
Rind of 2 lemons (pared with
    vegetable peeler)
Juice of 2 lemons
¾ cup sugar, divided

1 tablespoon dry white wine
    (optional)
2 egg yolks, beaten
4 egg whites
Lemon or lime slices

Blend cornstarch with ½ cup water. Combine remaining water, lemon peel, lemon juice, ¼ cup sugar, and wine, if desired; add to cornstarch mixture. Bring to a boil and cook until slightly thickened and clear. Remove from heat; add a little of the hot mixture to egg yolks and then add yolks to the soup, beating constantly. Remove peel if desired. Chill soup thoroughly. Beat egg whites until stiff; add remaining ½ cup sugar, a little at a time. Beat until whites form stiff, glossy peaks. Set aside a small amount of meringue for garnish and fold soup into remaining meringue. Serve immediately with dollops of meringue and lemon or lime slices. Yield: 6 to 8 servings.

ORANGE SOUP

3 cups (about 9 oranges)
    orange juice
6 tablespoons sugar
1½ tablespoons arrowroot
    moistened with 3
    tablespoons cold water

3 tablespoons or more
    Curaçao liqueur
3 ice cubes, crushed
1 large orange, divided into
    sections

Heat orange juice to boiling point; add sugar and moistened arrowroot. Stir for a moment over low heat until thickened. Remove from heat, cool, and add Curaçao. Refrigerate until ready to serve. Place crushed ice in 6 chilled bouillon cups and fill with cold soup. Garnish with orange sections and serve immediately. Yield: 6 servings.

COLD ORANGE SOUP

1 envelope unflavored gelatin
¼ cup hot water
¼ cup cold water
2 cups orange juice
¼ oup lomon juioe

1 tablespoon lime juice
¼ cup sugar or honey
1 cup diced orange sections
Fresh mint sprigs

Dissolve gelatin in hot water; add cold water, fruit juices, and sugar. Chill for several hours. Add orange sections before serving. Garnish with sprigs of mint. Yield: 4 servings.

ORIENTAL ORANGE SOUP

4 large oranges	¼ cup cornstarch
¾ cup firmly packed brown sugar	¼ cup water
	½ cup sherry
1 quart boiling water	Grapes

Peel and section oranges; remove seeds. Add sugar to boiling water in large saucepan, and stir until sugar is completely dissolved. Add orange sections with any juice that has accumulated. Combine cornstarch and water; add to orange mixture. Cook for 10 minutes, stirring gently to prevent lumping. Add sherry. Serve hot or cold with a few grapes in each serving. Yield: 4 to 5 servings.

PEACH AND PLUM SOUP

2 cups water	2 tablespoons cornstarch
1 cup fresh peach slices	1 tablespoon lemon juice
1 cup fresh plum slices	Fresh fruit
¼ to ½ cup sugar	

Bring water to a boil and simmer fruit slices for 15 to 20 minutes or until soft. Sieve; remove all liquid from pulp and discard pulp. Add sugar. Blend cornstarch with small amount of water; add to fruit mixture and quickly bring to a boil, stirring to prevent lumping. Stir in lemon juice. Serve cold with slices of fresh fruit. Yield: 4 to 5 servings.

SPICED PLUM SOUP

3 tablespoons whole cloves	1 teaspoon lemon juice
1 stick cinnamon, broken into 3 pieces	2 teaspoons grated lemon rind
	3 tablespoons honey
1 (16-ounce) jar purple plums, undrained and pitted	¼ teaspoon salt
	2 teaspoons cornstarch
2 cups cold water	½ cup plain yogurt
½ cup dry red wine	2 teaspoons dark brown sugar

Place cloves and cinnamon in a piece of cheesecloth; tie securely. Combine spice bag, plums, water, wine, lemon juice, lemon rind, honey, and salt in a saucepan; cook over medium heat 12 minutes. Remove and discard spice bag.

Remove plums from cooking liquid; put through a sieve, or puree in electric blender. Return pureed plums to cooking liquid.

Combine cornstarch and 2 tablespoons plum mixture, blending to a smooth paste; gradually stir into remaining plum mixture. Cook over medium heat until slightly thickened, stirring constantly. Chill thoroughly.

Combine yogurt and brown sugar, mixing well. Top each serving of soup with a heaping teaspoonful of yogurt mixture. Yield: 4 to 6 servings.

RASPBERRY FRUIT SOUP

2 tablespoons quick-cooking
   tapioca
¼ cup sugar
⅛ teaspoon salt
½ cup water
2 (10-ounce) packages frozen
   raspberries, thawed and
   undrained

⅓ cup lemon juice
1 tablespoon butter or
   margarine
½ cup whipping cream,
   whipped, or ½ cup
   commercial sour cream
Ground nutmeg

Combine tapioca, sugar, salt, water, and 1 package raspberries in saucepan. Cook, stirring constantly, over medium heat until mixture comes to a boil; reduce heat; simmer, uncovered, for 5 minutes.

Stir in lemon juice and butter; cool for 20 minutes. Add remaining package of raspberries, stirring to blend well. Chill. Serve in sherbet glasses. Top each serving with a dollop of whipped or sour cream; dust with nutmeg. Yield: 8 servings.

STRAWBERRY SOUP

2 (10-ounce) packages frozen
   strawberries, thawed
2 cups water
¼ cup sugar
1½ to 2 tablespoons
   quick-cooking tapioca

Dash of salt
1 tablespoon lemon juice
½ cup orange and grapefruit
   sections

Process strawberries in an electric blender until smooth, or press through a sieve; pour into a saucepan. Add water, sugar, tapioca, and salt; let stand 5 minutes.

Bring mixture to a boil over medium heat, stirring constantly. Remove from heat, and add lemon juice. Chill soup thoroughly.

Just before serving, stir in orange and grapefruit sections. Yield: 6 to 8 servings.

Photograph for this recipe on page 54

gumbos

Deep in South Louisiana's bayou country—where big-hearted, fun-loving people speak a mixture of French and English and where the food is as spicy as it is good—there originated a highly seasoned stewlike dish that made the Cajuns famous. They named it gumbo.

When the first Frenchmen settled South Louisiana, they lacked many of the ingredients to make their favorite stew, bouillabaisse. The Acadians of that area, or Cajuns, showed them how to use shrimp and crab in place of their Mediterranean fish; the Spanish settlers introduced them to spices, such as red pepper; while the Choctaw Indians taught them the value of filé powder (ground sassafras leaves). And from the Africans came *gombo*, or okra, the ingredient from which gumbo is named. The dish that resulted was better to many than the original bouillabaisse.

The key to a good gumbo, as any Cajun will quickly tell you, is in the roux. A roux is made by combining equal parts of flour and oil and cooking it over a slow fire until it turns the color of a dirty copper penny. It must be stirred constantly, for if the roux burns, it will ruin the entire gumbo.

Gumbo can be made with almost any kind of meat or fish. The most common ingredients are crab, shrimp, chicken, sausage, and game. But gumbo is always thickened with either okra or filé (fee-lay).

Okra gives gumbo a rich, earthy flavor and thickens the stew as it simmers. Filé powder, on the other hand, imparts a delicate flavor similar to that of thyme; a small amount can thicken a whole pot of gumbo.

Filé powder becomes stringy if it is allowed to boil, so it should be added only after the gumbo is completely cooked. Many people prefer to pass the filé at the table so each person can thicken the gumbo to his own liking.

CHICKEN GUMBO

1 (3-pound) chicken, cut up	1 (28-ounce) can whole
2 tablespoons melted butter or	tomatoes
margarine	1 cup uncooked regular rice
6 cups water, divided	1 tablespoon Worcestershire
1 medium onion, chopped	sauce
1 green pepper, diced	1 tablespoon salt
1 (16-ounce) can okra	¼ teaspoon pepper
1 (12-ounce) can whole	
kernel corn	

Brown chicken in butter in Dutch oven. Pour off drippings; reserve. Add 3 cups water to chicken; cover; simmer until tender, about 1½ hours. Sauté onion in reserved drippings until lightly browned. Add remaining ingredients; cover; cook for 1 hour, stirring occasionally. When chicken is tender, remove from stock; cut meat into small pieces and return to gumbo mixture. Cover; simmer, stirring occasionally, about 20 minutes or until hot. Yield: 6 to 8 servings.

CHICKEN FILÉ GUMBO

1 (3- or 4-pound) hen, cut	½ cup chopped green pepper
into serving pieces	2 quarts hot water
Salt and pepper to taste	1 cup chopped green onion
1 cup salad oil	tops
¼ cup all-purpose flour	½ cup chopped parsley
1 cup chopped onion	Gumbo filé to taste
1 cup chopped celery	Hot cooked rice

Season chicken with salt and pepper. Heat oil in Dutch oven. Add seasoned chicken and cook until golden brown. Remove chicken; add flour to make a roux. Add onion, celery, and green pepper, and cook slowly about 5 minutes or until soft. Add chicken and water; simmer until tender. Add green onion tops and parsley the last 15 or 20 minutes. When done, add filé (the powdered young leaves of sassafras used as a thickening agent and available, bottled, in most grocery stores). Serve with rice. Yield: 8 servings.

CHICKEN AND OKRA GUMBO

1 large onion, chopped	Salt
2 cups sliced okra, fresh or	Red and black pepper
frozen	2 quarts warm water
Salad oil or bacon drippings	Hot cooked rice
1 (2½- to 3-pound) chicken,	Gumbo filé
cut up	

Sauté onion and okra in ¼ cup salad oil over low heat about 30 minutes, stirring often. Season chicken with salt and pepper; brown chicken in additional salad oil in a heavy skillet. Pour off excess oil; add okra and onion mixture, and gradually stir in water.

Season gumbo to taste with salt and pepper. Cook over medium heat until chicken is tender (about 45 minutes). Remove bones from chicken, if desired. Serve gumbo over hot cooked rice, and thicken with gumbo filé. Yield: 8 to 10 servings.

CHICKEN-OYSTER GUMBO

1 (2½- to 3-pound) chicken, cut up	1 to 2 pints oysters, undrained
Salt	2 stalks celery, chopped
Red and black pepper	½ green pepper, chopped
½ cup salad oil	½ cup chopped parsley
¼ cup all purpose flour	½ cup chopped green onion tops
1 large or 2 medium onions, chopped	Hot cooked rice
2 quarts hot water	Gumbo filé

Season chicken with salt and pepper. Heat salad oil in a heavy iron pot; add chicken, and cook until browned. Remove chicken from pot, and stir flour into oil; cook over medium heat until a dark roux is formed, stirring constantly.

Add onion to roux, and cook until tender; add chicken. Gradually stir in hot water, blending well. Bring to a boil, and simmer until chicken is tender (about 1 hour). Remove chicken bones, if desired. Season to taste with salt and pepper.

Add oysters, celery, green pepper, parsley, and green onion to gumbo; simmer 20 minutes longer. Serve over rice. Thicken with gumbo filé, if desired. Yield: 8 to 10 servings.

CREOLE CHICKEN GUMBO

1 fryer chicken, cut up	2 tablespoons melted butter or margarine
2 cups water	2 (16-ounce) cans whole tomatoes
2 medium onions, sliced and divided	3 sprigs parsley, chopped
2 celery tops	½ teaspoon hot sauce
2 bay leaves	⅓ cup uncooked regular rice
1 teaspoon monosodium glutamate	½ pound okra, sliced
2 teaspoons salt, divided	1 teaspoon Creole seasoning
1 medium-size green pepper, chopped	1 teaspoon gumbo filé

Combine chicken, water, 1 onion, celery, bay leaves, monosodium gluta-mate, and 1 teaspoon salt in large kettle. Bring to boil, cover, and simmer for 40 minutes. Remove from heat, strain broth, and return to kettle. Remove meat from bones; cut into bite-size pieces and return to broth. Sauté remaining onion and green pepper in butter about 5 minutes. Add to chicken with 1 teaspoon salt, tomatoes, parsley, and hot sauce. Simmer for 20 minutes. Add rice and okra; simmer for 20 additional minutes. Remove from heat and stir in Creole seasoning and filé. Yield: 4 to 6 servings.

OKRA GUMBO

1 broiler-fryer chicken
2 (1-inch thick) slices ham
3 tablespoons melted
  margarine
1 onion, chopped
6 large tomatoes
1 pod red pepper, seeded
1 tablespoon chopped parsley
20 pods fresh okra, sliced or
1 (10-ounce) package
frozen, sliced okra

1 sprig thyme or 1 bay leaf
3 quarts water
Salt and pepper to taste
2 to 3 tablespoons all-purpose
  flour
Hot cooked rice

Cut up chicken; cut ham into small squares. Cook chicken and ham in margarine in covered kettle for 10 minutes. Add onion. Peel tomatoes and chop fine, straining off and reserving juice. Shred red pepper. Add tomatoes, pepper, parsley, okra, and thyme. Let cook until chicken is browned, stirring often. When well browned, add juice from tomatoes. Be careful not to let okra scorch.

When chicken is well fried and browned, add 3 quarts water and let simmer about 1 hour. Add salt and pepper. Remove from heat, remove chicken from bone, and return chicken to okra mixture. Mix flour with small amount of cold water; add to soup mixture. Stir well and heat until mixture thickens. Remove thyme. Serve over hot rice. Yield: 12 to 14 servings.

Photograph for this recipe on page 1

TURKEY GUMBO

2 small onions, diced
2 tablespoons melted butter
1 quart turkey broth (See
  Index under Chicken Broth)
2 cups canned tomatoes
4 cups sliced okra, cooked

2 cups chopped cooked turkey
2 tablespoons chopped parsley
½ teaspoon paprika
Salt and pepper to taste
2 cups hot cooked rice

Sauté onion in butter until tender but not brown. Add broth, tomatoes, okra, turkey, parsley, and paprika. Simmer for 10 minutes and season to taste. Add cooked rice. Heat and serve. Yield: 4 to 6 servings.

TURKEY AND SAUSAGE GUMBO

1 turkey carcass
½ cup salad oil
½ cup all-purpose flour
1½ large onions, chopped
½ green pepper, chopped
1 stalk celery, chopped
1½ pounds smoked sausage,
   cut into 2½-inch pieces

Salt
Red and black pepper
¼ cup chopped parsley
¼ cup chopped green onion
   tops
Hot cooked rice
Gumbo filé (optional)

Use a turkey carcass with a little meat left on it; a smoked one is best. Cover carcass with water, and boil until meat leaves bones (about 1 hour). Reserve broth, and remove meat from carcass; discard bones.

Combine salad oil and flour in a large iron pot; cook over medium heat, stirring constantly, until a medium roux is formed. Add onion, green pepper, and celery; cook about 5 minutes or until tender, stirring constantly. Add sausage, turkey, and 2 to 3 quarts broth (add water to make 2 quarts, if necessary); simmer 1 hour.

Season gumbo to taste with salt and pepper. Stir in parsley and green onion; cook 10 minutes longer. Serve over rice. Thicken with gumbo filé, if desired. Yield: 8 to 10 servings.

DUCK AND SAUSAGE GUMBO

1 cup salad oil
1 cup all-purpose flour
1 large onion, chopped
2 (2- to 2½-pound) wild
   ducks or 1 (5-pound)
   domestic duck, cut up
Salt
Black and cayenne pepper
2 pounds smoked sausage, cut
   into 2-inch pieces

2 quarts warm water
1½ to 2 tablespoons hot
   pepper sauce
¼ cup chopped parsley
¼ cup chopped green onion
   tops
Hot cooked rice
Gumbo filé

Combine oil and flour in a heavy iron pot; cook over medium heat, stirring constantly, until a medium roux is formed. Add onion; cook about 5 minutes longer, stirring constantly.

Season duck with salt and pepper; add to roux. Cook about 10 minutes, stirring frequently; add sausage, and cook 5 minutes longer. Add water gradually, mixing well; bring to a boil. Reduce heat, and simmer until duck is tender (about 2 hours).

Season gumbo to taste with salt and pepper; add pepper sauce, parsley, and green onion. Cook 5 minutes longer.

Before serving, skim fat off top; remove bones from duck, if desired. Serve over rice, and thicken with gumbo filé. Yield: 8 to 10 servings.

Note: Duck and Oyster Gumbo can be made by substituting 1 pint oysters for the sausage; add oysters the last 20 minutes of cooking. Delicious served with French bread and red wine.

DUCK GUMBO

2 or 3 ducks
Salt and pepper to taste
¼ cup all-purpose flour
¼ cup salad oil
1 large onion, finely chopped
1 large green pepper, finely
  chopped

¼ cup all-purpose flour
2 to 3 cups water (from
  cooking giblets)
Hot cooked rice

Cut up ducks for frying. Boil giblets in a large amount of water and set aside. Season ducks with salt and pepper and dredge each piece in ¼ cup flour; brown in hot oil. Remove from oil. Add onion and green pepper and cook until soft; remove from oil. Make a roux by adding ¼ cup flour to oil and cooking until very dark brown. Add water from giblets. Return onion, pepper, and duck to roux and cook at very low temperature about 2 hours. Serve over hot rice. Yield: 6 to 8 servings.

SEAFOOD GUMBO

1 cup salad oil or bacon
  drippings
1 cup all-purpose flour
2 large onions, chopped
2 stalks celery, chopped
1 large green pepper, chopped
6 cloves garlic, minced
1 gallon warm water
4 cups sliced okra
3 tomatoes, peeled and
  chopped
2 tablespoons salt
Red and black pepper to taste

1 pint oysters, undrained
1 dozen cleaned fresh crabs*
  with claws or 1 pound fresh
  or frozen crabmeat
1½ to 2 pounds fresh or
  frozen medium shrimp,
  peeled and deveined
½ cup chopped parsley
½ cup chopped green onion
  tops
Hot cooked rice
Gumbo filé (optional)

Combine oil and flour in a heavy pot over medium heat; cook, stirring constantly, until roux is the color of a copper penny (about 10 to 15 minutes). Add onion, celery, green pepper, and garlic to roux; cook, stirring constantly, until vegetables are tender. Do not let roux burn as it will ruin gumbo; reduce heat, if necessary.

Gradually add 1 gallon warm water to roux, in small amounts at first, blending well after each addition; add okra and tomatoes. Bring mixture to a boil. Reduce heat; simmer, stirring occasionally, at least 20 minutes (1 to 1½ hours is better as the roux develops more flavor at this point). Stir in salt, pepper, and seafood.

Bring gumbo to a boil, and simmer 10 minutes. Add parsley and green onion; simmer 5 minutes longer. Remove from heat, and serve the gumbo over hot rice.

Gumbo can be further thickened, if desired, by adding a small amount of filé to each serving. Yield: 12 to 14 servings.

*To clean fresh crabs: Pour scalding water over crabs to kill them; remove large claws, and wash thoroughly. Turn crab upside down and lift the long, tapered point (the apron); pull off shell and remove the soft, spongy mass. Remove and discard legs. Wash crab thoroughly, and break body in half lengthwise; add to gumbo along with claws.

Note: Almost any kind of meat, poultry, or game can be substituted for the seafood in this recipe. Just cut it into pieces and brown it before adding to the roux.

Photograph for this recipe on page 64

SEAFOOD-HAM GUMBO

1¼ to 2 pounds fresh shrimp	1 (16-ounce) can whole
½ teaspoon crab boil	tomatoes
seasoning	1 large green pepper, chopped
2 tablespoons bacon drippings	1 pound crabmeat
2 tablespoons all-purpose flour	1 clove garlic, crushed
1 large onion, chopped	1 teaspoon salt
1 cup cooked, chopped ham	½ teaspoon freshly ground
2 pounds fresh okra, sliced or	black pepper
1 (10-ounce) package	¼ teaspoon thyme
frozen sliced okra	¼ teaspoon oregano
3 stalks celery, chopped	2 bay leaves
2 tablespoons chopped parsley	Hot cooked rice

Cover shrimp with water and add crab boil; cook until shrimp are tender, about 10 minutes. Drain and reserve water. Peel shrimp and reserve. In an iron pot or Dutch oven, make a roux with bacon drippings and flour. Add onion and sauté until transparent. Add ham and okra. Cook about 10 minutes over medium heat, stirring constantly. Add shrimp water, celery, parsley, tomatoes, green pepper, crabmeat, garlic, salt, and pepper. Simmer mixture for 1 hour. Add thyme, oregano, bay leaves, and peeled shrimp. Cook for an additional 20 minutes. Remove bay leaves and serve over rice. This can be frozen. Yield: 8 to 10 servings.

QUICK CRAB GUMBO

1 (7-ounce) can crabmeat	Freshly ground pepper to taste
1 (16-ounce) can stewed	1 teaspoon salt
tomatoes	¼ teaspoon dried thyme
1 (16-ounce) can okra	2 cups hot cooked rice
7 or 8 dashes of hot pepper	Paprika (optional)
sauce	

Combine ingredients, except rice and paprika, in saucepan, and cook until boiling. Serve in soup bowls, and place a large mound of cooked rice in center of each serving. If desired, sprinkle rice mounds with paprika. Yield: 2 to 3 servings.

MIXED SHELLFISH GUMBO

6 tablespoons olive oil, divided

1¼ cups finely chopped onion, divided

¼ cup finely chopped green pepper

3 cloves garlic, divided

Pinch of saffron

1 cup uncooked regular rice

1¾ cups water

Salt

Black pepper

⅛ teaspoon dried red pepper

1 teaspoon crushed oregano

1½ cups peeled, diced tomato

1½ cups dry white wine

18 small clams (optional)

2 (12-ounce) cans oysters, drained

½ pound shrimp, cooked and shelled

1 pound scallops, halved

Heat 2 tablespoons oil in a large saucepan, and add ¼ cup onion, green pepper, and 1 clove minced garlic; sauté until soft. Add saffron, and cook 2 minutes. Stir in rice, water, 1 teaspoon salt, and ¼ teaspoon black pepper. Bring to a boil, and reduce heat. Cover and simmer 17 minutes or until rice is tender. Set aside and keep warm.

Heat remaining ¼ cup oil in a Dutch oven; add 1 cup onion and 2 cloves minced garlic; sauté until soft. Stir in 1½ teaspoons salt, ½ teaspoon black pepper, red pepper, oregano, tomato, wine, and seafood. Cook over medium heat about 5 minutes. Serve over rice. Yield: about 8 servings.

CREOLE SHRIMP GUMBO

1 ham hock

3 quarts water

¼ cup bacon drippings

1 stalk celery, chopped

4 large green peppers, chopped

4 large onions, chopped

4 cloves garlic, minced

2 pounds okra, sliced

½ bunch parsley, chopped

4 (16-ounce) cans whole tomatoes

2 tablespoons salt

2 tablespoons Worcestershire sauce

1 tablespoon paprika

3 bay leaves

1 (6-ounce) can tomato paste

½ teaspoon pepper

1 tablespoon sugar

Hot sauce to taste

2½ teaspoons thyme

2 pounds fresh shrimp, cooked and peeled

1 tablespoon gumbo filé

Hot cooked rice

Put ham hock into water and let simmer for 30 minutes. Put bacon drippings into heavy skillet. Add celery, peppers, onions, garlic, okra, and parsley; cook slowly for 20 minutes. Add to pot containing ham.

Add tomatoes, salt, Worcestershire, paprika, bay leaves, tomato paste, pepper, sugar, hot sauce, and thyme to ham; let simmer for 3 hours. At end of 3 hours, remove meat from ham bone and add meat to liquid. Remove bay leaves. Add shrimp and cook slowly for a few minutes. Just before serving, stir in filé. Serve over rice. Yield: 8 to 10 servings.

QUICK-AND-EASY OYSTER GUMBO

¼ cup all-purpose flour
¼ cup melted bacon drippings, butter, or margarine
1 cup chopped green pepper
1 cup chopped onion
1 clove garlic, crushed
2 to 3 cups water
2 tablespoons chopped parsley
1½ teaspoons salt

¼ teaspoon pepper
¼ teaspoon ground thyme
Dash of cayenne pepper
1 bay leaf
½ pound peeled, deveined shrimp
1 pint oyster, undrained
Hot cooked rice
Gumbo filé (optional)

Combine flour and bacon drippings in a heavy saucepan or Dutch oven; cook over medium heat, stirring constantly, until roux is the color of a copper penny (about 10 to 15 minutes). (Do not let roux burn as it will ruin the gumbo; reduce heat, if necessary.)

Add green pepper, onion, and garlic to the roux; cook, stirring constantly, until vegetables are tender. Add water, parsley, and seasonings; simmer 30 minutes. Add shrimp and oysters; bring to a boil, and cook 5 minutes. Serve over rice. Add filé to each serving to thicken, if desired. Yield: 4 servings.

Note: Chicken may be substituted for shrimp, if desired. Cut chicken into bite-size pieces; brown in hot salad oil, and add to roux.

OKRA GUMBO WITH CRAB AND SHRIMP

3 slices bacon
2 pounds raw shrimp, peeled and deveined
¾ cup chopped onion
3 cloves garlic, crushed
2 (10-ounce) packages frozen whole okra
1 (8-ounce) can tomato sauce
1 (16-ounce) can whole tomatoes, undrained

2 tablespoons seafood seasoning (crab or shrimp boil)
Salt
4 live hard-shell crabs
½ teaspoon gumbo filé
Hot cooked rice

Fry bacon until crisp; drain on paper towels, and set aside. Reserve drippings. Measure 2 tablespoons bacon drippings into Dutch oven. Add shrimp, onion, and garlic; sauté until onion is tender and shrimp are pink. Cut okra into 1-inch pieces, and add with tomato sauce, tomatoes, seafood seasoning, 1½ teaspoons salt, and 5 cups water to shrimp mixture. Bring to a boil; reduce heat, and simmer, covered, for 1 hour. Bring 1 quart water and 1 tablespoon salt to boiling in large saucepan. Place crabs in colander; wash in cold water until clean. Plunge crabs headfirst into boiling water; bring water to boiling again. Reduce heat, and simmer, covered, for 10 minutes. Drain; let cool; cut each in half. Add crabs to okra mixture. Simmer for 30 additional minutes. Add filé. Remove from heat; crumble bacon over top. Serve with rice. Yield: 8 servings.

meat &
poultry soups

On crisp, cold days, there is nothing quite as appealing as a piping hot bowl of soup. These are as satisfying as they are warming, a meal in themselves since they are chock full of meat and vegetables.

Some owe their meaty flavor to beef, while others begin with sausage or chicken. Many are thick with vegetables and all are skillfully seasoned. The combinations of ingredients used in making soups are as varied as people's tastes.

As long as you have some kind of meat or broth and fresh, canned, or frozen vegetables, a simmering pot of soup is there for the making.

BEEF SOUP

1 pound ground round beef	1 large onion, chopped
Salt and pepper to taste	1½ cups sliced carrot.
1½ teaspoons Italian	1½ cups sliced celery
seasoning, divided	⅓ cup chopped parsley
2 quarts water	Grated Romano cheese

Season ground beef with salt and pepper and ½ teaspoon Italian seasoning. Mix well and shape into small balls about the size of marbles. Put into a heavy pot with water and bring to a boil. Add all vegetables, parsley, and the additional teaspoon Italian seasoning. Add more salt and pepper if needed. Cover and cook over low heat about 2 hours. Serve sprinkled with Romano cheese. Yield: 6 to 8 servings.

BEEF-VEGETABLE SOUP

1 (2½- to 3-pound) chuck roast, cut into cubes	1 cup lima beans
1 gallon water	1 cup cut green beans
1 tablespoon salt	1 cup peas
½ head cabbage, chopped	1 (12-ounce) can whole kernel corn, drained
1½ cups chopped onion	3 to 4 potatoes, cubed
6 carrots, cut into 1-inch pieces	2 tablespoons chopped parsley
¾ cup chopped celery	1 (6-ounce) can tomato paste or ¾ cup catsup
¼ cup chopped green pepper	
1 (28-ounce) can whole tomatoes, chopped and undrained	

Combine roast, water, and salt in a large saucepan or Dutch oven; cover and bring to a boil. Add cabbage, onion, carrots, celery, green pepper, and tomatoes; return to a boil. Lower heat; cover and simmer 30 minutes. Add remaining ingredients; cover and simmer 3½ hours. Yield: 12 to 15 servings.

Photograph for this recipe on page 77

BEEF BRISKET SOUP

2 pounds beef brisket	1 large onion, chopped
2 quarts water	½ cup shredded American or Cheddar cheese
1 tablespoon salt	
5 medium potatoes, peeled and diced	⅔ cup oatmeal, uncooked
Dash of celery salt	1 (16-ounce) can cream-style corn (optional)

Cut brisket into pieces; simmer, covered, in salted water. When meat is tender, add potatoes, celery salt, onion, cheese, and oatmeal. Add corn, if desired. Continue to cook, covered, until vegetables are done, stirring once or twice while cooking. Remove from heat and serve in separate small bowls, allowing a piece of beef for each bowl. Yield: 8 servings.

CORNED BEEF SOUP

1 (12-ounce) can corned beef, cubed

2 (16-ounce) cans mixed vegetables, undrained

1 (17-ounce) can cream-style corn

1 (16-ounce) can whole tomatoes, undrained

1 large onion, chopped

2 potatoes, peeled and cubed

3 beef bouillon cubes

1 teaspoon chili powder

Salt and pepper to taste

2 cups water

Combine all ingredients in a large pot; simmer for 1 to 1½ hours or until potatoes are tender. Yield: 12 to 14 servings.

CORNED BEEF-VEGETABLE SOUP

1 (46-ounce) can tomato juice
1 (17-ounce) can green peas,
   undrained
1 (17-ounce) can cream-style
   corn
1 (12-ounce) can corned beef,
   chopped

1 cup water
Salt and pepper to taste
½ to 1 cup uncooked elbow
   macaroni

Combine all ingredients except macaroni in a Dutch oven; bring to a boil, and simmer 20 minutes. Add macaroni; simmer 8 to 10 minutes or until macaroni is just tender, stirring occasionally. Yield: 8 to 10 servings.

MEXICALI SOUP

¼ pound ground beef
¾ teaspoon chili powder,
   divided
¼ teaspoon salt
Dash of black pepper
2 tablespoons minced onion

1 tablespoon margarine
1 (10½-ounce) can tomato
   soup, undiluted
1 soup can water

Combine beef, ½ teaspoon chili powder, salt, and pepper; shape into 12 small balls. In saucepan, brown meatballs and onion in margarine. Add soup, remaining ¼ teaspoon chili powder, and water. Simmer about 5 minutes. Yield: 2 to 3 servings.

HAMBURGER SOUP

2 pounds ground beef
2 tablespoons olive oil or
   salad oil
½ teaspoon salt
¼ teaspoon pepper
¼ teaspoon oregano
¼ teaspoon basil
⅛ teaspoon savory
1 (1⅜-ounce) envelope onion
   soup mix

6 cups boiling water
1 (8-ounce) can tomato sauce
1 tablespoon soy sauce
1 cup diagonally sliced celery
¼ cup diced celery leaves
1 cup sliced carrot
⅓ cup dried split peas
1 cup elbow macaroni,
   uncooked
Grated Parmesan cheese

Brown meat in oil in a large saucepan with a tight fitting lid. Add salt, pepper, oregano, basil, savory, and onion soup mix. Stir in boiling water, tomato sauce, and soy sauce. Cover and simmer about 15 minutes. Add celery, celery leaves, and carrot to simmering mixture and continue to cook for 30 minutes. Add peas and macaroni and simmer for 30 additional minutes, adding more water if necessary. Top with Parmesan cheese to serve. Yield: 6 to 8 servings.

MEATBALL SOUP

1 pound ground round steak
½ cup soft breadcrumbs
2 tablespoons milk
2 teaspoons instant minced
  onion
¼ teaspoon pepper
½ teaspoon garlic salt
1 teaspoon Worcestershire
  sauce

2 teaspoons salt, divided
2 quarts water
2 (8-ounce) cans tomato
  sauce
2 beef bouillon cubes
1 teaspoon savory
¼ cup alphabet macaroni

Combine ground meat, breadcrumbs, milk, onion, pepper, garlic salt, Worcestershire sauce, and 1 teaspoon salt. Shape into small balls about 1 inch in diameter. Bring water to a boil in a large saucepan. Stir in tomato sauce, bouillon cubes, savory, remaining 1 teaspoon salt, and macaroni. Drop in meatballs and simmer slowly about 30 minutes. Serve immediately, or chill and then skim off any fat that solidifies on top before reheating. Yield: 6 servings.

Photograph for this recipe on page 74

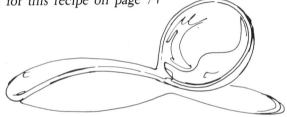

MAGHERITSA (GREEK EASTER SOUP)

3 pounds spring lamb (shin
  and shoulder)
1 lamb liver
1 gallon water
1 teaspoon salt
¾ cup uncooked regular rice
1 onion, finely chopped
1 tablespoon water
¼ cup salad oil

4 or 5 green onions, chopped
  (tops included)
2 tablespoons chopped parsley
½ teaspoon dried mint
¼ cup chopped fresh dillweed
Salt and pepper to taste
3 eggs, beaten
Juice of 2 lemons

Boil lamb and liver in salted water about 1 hour or until tender. Remove meat from broth and cut into small pieces. Skim fat from broth and add enough water to make 3 quarts; add rice and simmer for 15 minutes.

Sauté onion in 1 tablespoon water and salad oil until lightly browned; add green onions, parsley, mint, and dillweed. Sauté for 15 minutes.

Add meat, onion mixture, salt, and pepper to rice and broth; simmer about 15 minutes. Remove from heat.

Combine eggs and lemon juice; heat thoroughly until well blended. Slowly add 2 cups hot soup to egg-lemon mixture, beating constantly; gradually stir mixture into soup. Heat to boiling point and remove from heat immediately. Yield: 10 to 12 servings.

HAM 'N' CORN SOUP

3 quarts water
2 pounds cooked ham, cubed
2 medium onions, chopped
1 (16-ounce) can stewed
   tomatoes
1 large green pepper, chopped

1 (10-ounce) package frozen
   corn
½ teaspoon pepper
½ teaspoon sugar
Salt to taste

Combine water, ham, onions, tomatoes, and green pepper in a large saucepan; place over heat and simmer about 1 hour. Add corn, pepper, sugar, and salt; simmer 10 to 15 minutes. Yield: 6 servings.

HAM AND VEGETABLE SOUP

1½ pounds meaty ham hock
2 (28-ounce) cans whole
   tomatoes
1 (8-ounce) can tomato sauce
4 potatoes, diced
1 cup uncooked elbow
   macaroni
1 cup chopped celery
4 carrots, sliced
½ cup chopped green pepper
1 teaspoon celery seeds

1 tablespoon salt
3 bay leaves
1 teaspoon pepper
1 dried chili pepper, crumbled
Garlic salt to taste
2 cups yellow whole kernel
   corn
2 cups baby lima beans
2 cups cut green beans
2 cups green peas

Cover ham hock with water in a large saucepan or Dutch oven. Add tomatoes and tomato sauce; bring to boil. Add next 11 ingredients; cover and simmer about 1 hour. Add remaining ingredients; simmer about 45 minutes.

Remove ham hock and bay leaves from soup. Remove meat from ham hock; chop meat and return to soup. Yield: 10 to 12 servings.

HOT AND SOUR SOUP

1 quart chicken broth
1 teaspoon salt
1 tablespoon soy sauce
4 Chinese mushrooms,
   shredded
½ cup bamboo shoots
½ cup shredded pork
4 ounces bean curd, shredded

¼ teaspoon white pepper
2 tablespoons vinegar
2 tablespoons cornstarch
3 tablespoons water
1 egg, slightly beaten
2 teaspoons sesame oil
1 green onion, finely chopped

Combine chicken broth, salt, soy sauce, mushrooms, bamboo shoots, and pork in a 3-quart saucepan. Bring to a boil; reduce heat. Cover and simmer 3 minutes. Add bean curd, pepper, and vinegar, stirring well; return to a boil.

Combine cornstarch and water; add to soup, and cook, stirring constantly, until thickened. Slowly add egg, stirring constantly. Remove from heat; stir in sesame oil, and sprinkle onion on top. Yield: about 6 servings.

PORTUGUESE SOUP

1½ pounds Portuguese or
   Polish sausage, sliced
5 cups water, divided
2 (15-ounce) cans kidney
   beans, drained
2 carrots, diced
½ head cabbage, coarsely
   chopped

1 medium onion, chopped
2 medium potatoes, diced
½ green pepper, chopped
1 clove garlic, finely chopped
1 (8-ounce) can tomato sauce

Simmer sausage in 2 cups water 30 to 45 minutes. Add remaining ingredients, and simmer 1 to 1½ hours. Yield: 10 servings.

SKI-SLOPE SOUP

1 pound bulk sausage
2 (15-ounce) cans kidney
   beans
1 (14½-ounce) can whole
   tomatoes
1 large onion, chopped
1 quart water

1½ teaspoons seasoned salt
½ teaspoon garlic salt
½ teaspoon thyme leaves
2 bay leaves
⅛ teaspoon pepper
1 cup diced potato

Brown sausage; drain well. Combine all ingredients except potatoes in a 4-quart saucepan or Dutch oven. Cover and simmer 1 hour. Add potatoes, and cook 20 minutes. Discard bay leaves.

Beat soup with rotary beater until all the ingredients are well shredded (about 3 minutes). Yield: 8 to 10 servings.

CHICKEN BISQUE

2 tablespoons butter or
   margarine
2 tablespoons all-purpose flour
1 cup ground cooked chicken

3 cups chicken broth
1 cup half-and-half, scalded
Salt and pepper
Chopped parsley (optional)

Melt butter in a heavy saucepan; blend in flour, and cook until bubbly. Add chicken and broth; cook, stirring constantly, until mixture boils. Reduce heat; stir in half-and-half. Season to taste with salt and pepper. Serve immediately. Garnish with parsley, if desired. Yield: 4 servings.

CHICKEN GIBLET AND BARLEY SOUP

2 pounds chicken wings,
necks, backs, hearts, and
gizzards
2 quarts water
2 medium carrots, coarsely
chopped
2 stalks celery, coarsely
chopped

1 small onion, pierced with 2
cloves
1 tablespoon salt
Dash of pepper
½ pound fresh mushrooms,
coarsely chopped
½ cup barley
2 tablespoons chopped parsley

Cook chicken in water with carrots, celery, onion, salt, and pepper; simmer 30 minutes. Add mushrooms and barley; cover, and simmer for 1 hour or until barley is tender. Remove chicken; debone and dice. Add chicken and parsley to soup. Remove onion. Yield: 8 to 10 servings.

CHICKEN NOODLE-CRESS SOUP

1 quart seasoned chicken
broth (See Index)
½ cup finely diced carrot
¼ bunch watercress

½ cup finely diced chicken
1 cup cooked, fine egg
noodles

To hot broth add carrot, watercress stems cut into ⅛-inch lengths, and chicken. Cook over medium heat for 10 minutes. Add noodles and coarsely cut watercress leaves. Heat thoroughly and serve immediately. Yield: 4 to 5 servings.

CHICKEN VEGETABLE SOUP

1 (3- to 3½-pound)
broiler-fryer, cut up
1 cup chopped celery and
leaves
1 cup coarsely chopped onion
½ cup thinly sliced carrots
1 (28-ounce) can whole
tomatoes or 3½ cups
peeled, chopped fresh
tomatoes
3 cups water
3 chicken bouillon cubes
2 tablespoons chopped fresh
parsley

4 whole cloves
6 whole peppercorns
1 small bay leaf
2 teaspoons salt
3 tablespoons uncooked
regular rice
2 cups skim milk
2 tablespoons dry sherry
(optional)
1 lemon, thinly sliced, or 2
tablespoons lemon juice
2 tablespoons chopped fresh
parsley

Combine first 13 ingredients in a large Dutch oven. Cover and simmer 1 hour or until chicken is well done.

Remove from heat, and let cool slightly. Remove skin and bones from chicken, and cut meat into bite-size pieces. Set aside.

Pour broth (in several batches) into container of electric blender; process until smooth. Return broth to Dutch oven. Stir in milk and chicken; add sherry, if desired. Heat slowly; do not allow to boil. Just before serving, garnish with lemon slices and 2 tablespoons parsley. Yield: about 6 servings.

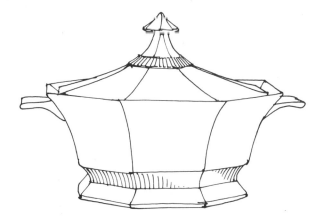

COUNTRY-STYLE CHICKEN SOUP

1 (4-pound) stewing chicken, cut into pieces	½ teaspoon poultry seasoning
1 cup chopped onion	1 egg
1 carrot, peeled and quartered	1 tablespoon chopped parsley
1 bay leaf	2 carrots, peeled
1 teaspoon salt	2 stalks celery
2 quarts water	¼ cup chicken fat
½ cup fresh breadcrumbs	⅓ cup all-purpose flour
½ teaspoon salt	1 cup milk

Place chicken in a large heavy pot with onion, quartered carrot, bay leaf, 1 teaspoon salt, and water; simmer for 2 to 3 hours, or until tender; remove chicken and chill stock. Remove chicken from bones; discard skin; reserve 1 cup chicken for soup. (Chill remainder to use for salad, casserole, or other chicken dish.) Grind 1 cup chicken; add breadcrumbs, ½ teaspoon salt, poultry seasoning, egg, and parsley; blend. Form firmly into small balls; set aside. Remove layer of fat from chilled stock; reserve. Heat chicken stock (there should be 4 cups). Cut carrots and celery into matchstick-size pieces; add to stock; cook for 10 to 15 minutes, or until tender. Melt ¼ cup chicken fat in saucepan; blend in flour; add milk slowly, stirring constantly. Pour mixture slowly into stock; cook, stirring constantly, until mixture is thickened. Drop chicken balls into soup; heat for 5 minutes more; serve. Yield: 4 to 6 servings.

CURRIED CHICKEN SOUP

½ cup diced celery	1 to 1½ teaspoons curry
¼ cup minced onion	powder
¼ cup melted butter	1 quart milk
¼ cup all-purpose flour	2 cups diced cooked chicken
1 teaspoon salt	¼ cup chopped parsley or
⅛ teaspoon pepper	toasted coconut

Sauté celery and onion in butter over low heat until tender. Blend in flour and seasonings. Add milk, and cook, stirring constantly, until smooth and thickened. Add chicken and heat thoroughly. Serve in hot bowls. Garnish with a sprig of parsley or toasted coconut. Yield: 6 servings.

CURRIED CHICKEN NOODLE SOUP

1 medium-size green pepper, chopped	Salt and pepper to taste
½ medium onion, finely diced	1 cup uncooked narrow egg noodles
½ cup diced celery	Boiling salted water
2 cloves garlic, finely chopped	1 cup diced cooked chicken
3 tablespoons melted butter or margarine	1 (8¼-ounce) can pineapple tidbits, drained
2 quarts chicken broth	2 tablespoons chopped pimiento
½ teaspoon curry powder	¼ cup sherry
⅛ teaspoon hot sauce	
½ teaspoon Worcestershire sauce	

Sauté green pepper, onion, celery, and garlic in melted butter just until tender. Add chicken broth and seasonings; simmer about 10 minutes.

Cook noodles in boiling salted water until tender; drain and add to broth mixture. Add chicken, pineapple, pimiento, and sherry; simmer 10 minutes longer. Yield: 10 servings.

OLIVE CREAM OF CHICKEN SOUP

2 quarts chicken broth (See Index)	⅓ cup all-purpose flour
½ teaspoon ground thyme	1½ cups milk
½ cup chopped onion	½ cup sliced pimiento-stuffed green olives
1 cup grated carrot	2 tablespoons chopped parsley
2 cups diced cooked chicken	Salt and pepper to taste

Heat chicken broth to boiling. Add thyme, onion, carrot, and chicken. Cover and cook until onion is tender. Combine flour and milk; mix until smooth and add to chicken mixture. Cook over low heat until thickened, stirring constantly. Add olives, parsley, salt, and pepper. Yield: 10 to 12 servings.

ROSEMARY SOUP

1 (5-pound) hen	2 teaspoons salt
1 carrot, sliced	2 quarts water
1 medium onion, sliced	½ teaspoon rosemary, crushed
2 celery tops	1 tablespoon quick-cooking tapioca
6 sprigs parsley	Pepper to taste
1 bay leaf	
4 whole cloves	

Combine first 9 ingredients in a Dutch oven, and bring to a boil. Cover and simmer 35 to 45 minutes or until chicken is tender. Remove chicken from broth, and reserve chicken for use in other recipes.

Strain broth, and return to Dutch oven. Add rosemary, and simmer 20 minutes. Strain and cool; skim off fat. Stir tapioca and pepper into broth; heat thoroughly. Yield: 8 to 10 servings.

CREAM OF TURKEY

1 small onion, diced	2½ cups water
2 tablespoons melted butter or margarine	1 (1½-ounce) envelope turkey noodle soup mix
2 tablespoons all-purpose flour	½ cup half-and-half or milk

Sauté onion in butter in medium-size saucepan until tender. Blend in flour; gradually stir in water and bring to a boil. Stir in soup mix; cover and cook for 10 minutes, stirring occasionally. Blend in half-and-half. Do not boil. Yield: 4 servings.

seafood soups

No area is more graciously endowed with an abundance of fresh seafood than is the South. With such a tremendous variety of fish and shellfish to choose from, it is no wonder that our chapter on seafood soups abounds with such appetizing and satisfying soups.

All sorts of delicacies come to mind when seafood is mentioned—shrimp, crab, clams, oysters, scallops, and many kinds of fish. Our collection of recipes proves that the ways to enjoy fish and shellfish soups are equally varied.

Many of these soups contain a broth, tomato, or cream base and are delicately seasoned with herbs. A subtle blending of flavors occurs when the natural seafood juices simmer with carefully selected ingredients. You'll want to try many of these recipes.

CLAM AND CHICKEN SOUP

2 (10¾-ounce) cans
   condensed cream of
   chicken soup, undiluted
2 (10¾-ounce) cans
   condensed consommé,
   undiluted

2 medium onions, chopped
2 (4-ounce) cans minced
   clams, drained, juice
   reserved

Combine soup, consommé, onions, and clam juice in top of double boiler. Simmer for 20 minutes. Add clams last and cook just long enough to heat thoroughly. Yield: 8 servings.

CLAM MONGOLE

1 (11½-ounce) can condensed
   green pea soup, undiluted
1 (10¾-ounce) can condensed
   tomato soup, undiluted
1 (10¾-ounce) can condensed
   cream of mushroom soup,
   undiluted

1 (7-ounce) can minced
   clams, undrained
2 cups half-and-half
1 tablespoon cooking sherry
   (optional)
Chopped parsley

Combine soups, clams, and half-and-half; simmer 5 minutes. Add sherry; mix well. Garnish with chopped parsley. Serve immediately. Yield: 5 servings.

CLAM AND OYSTER BISQUE

1 pound clams
2 cups oysters
½ cup butter or margarine
2 strips bacon, chopped
¾ teaspoon chopped parsley
½ cup chopped onion
⅓ cup chopped green pepper
1 medium potato, peeled and
   diced
¼ cup chopped celery

2 small carrots, peeled and
   chopped
1 teaspoon salt
¼ teaspoon pepper
Thyme to taste
6 dashes of hot sauce
½ teaspoon Worcestershire
   sauce
3 cups half-and-half, scalded
3 cups water

Combine clams, oysters, butter, bacon, parsley and vegetables in a large saucepan; simmer 50 minutes.

Pour mixture into container of electric blender; process until smooth. Return to saucepan, and stir in remaining ingredients. Heat thoroughly. Serve immediately. Yield: about 10 to 12 servings.

CRAB BISQUE

1½ tablespoons butter or
  margarine
1½ tablespoons all-purpose
  flour
3 cups half-and-half
½ cup whipping cream
2 tablespoons diced celery

1 (6½-ounce) can crab,
  drained and flaked
½ teaspoon salt
Pepper to taste
2 tablespoons sherry
Paprika

Melt butter in a heavy saucepan; blend in flour, and cook until bubbly. Gradually stir in half-and-half; cook over low heat, stirring constantly, until slightly thickened. Add whipping cream, celery, crab, salt, pepper, and sherry. Heat thoroughly, stirring frequently. Garnish with paprika. Yield: about 4 servings.

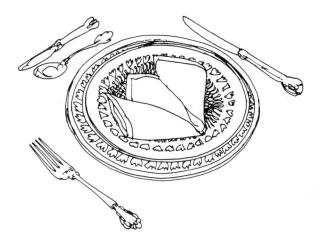

CREAMY SHE-CRAB SOUP

2 leeks
1 onion
8 stalks celery
½ cup butter
2 tablespoons all-purpose flour
1 teaspoon tomato paste
⅛ teaspoon whole oregano
1 quart chicken broth (See
  Index)

1 quart fish stock (See Index)
4 ounces crab roe
½ pound crabmeat
¼ cup sherry
1 teaspoon Worcestershire
  sauce
Salt and pepper to taste
2 egg yolks, beaten
1 cup whipping cream

Dice vegetables. Melt butter; add vegetables and sauté until tender. Add flour, tomato paste, and oregano; stir well. Stir in chicken broth and fish stock, and boil for 30 minutes, stirring occasionally. Add crab roe, crabmeat, sherry, Worcestershire sauce, salt, and pepper. Cook for 5 minutes and remove from heat. Add egg yolks and cream. Serve at once. Yield: 18 to 20 servings.

SHE-CRAB SOUP

1 medium onion, chopped	¼ pound crab roe
3 tablespoons butter, divided	⅛ teaspoon white pepper
2 teaspoons all-purpose flour	⅛ teaspoon ground mace
6 cups milk, divided	½ cup sherry
1 pound (or 2 cups) flaked,	Commercial sour cream
white crabmeat	Parsley sprigs or paprika

Sauté onion in 1½ tablespoons butter over low heat. Melt rest of butter in top of double boiler and blend in flour. Stir in onion and add 4 cups milk, stirring constantly. Add crabmeat and roe and stir well; add pepper and mace and cook slowly for 20 minutes. Add 2 cups milk and stir well. Remove from heat and add sherry. Serve in soup bowls which have been heated, top with a dollop of sour cream, and garnish with parsley sprigs or a sprinkle of paprika. Yield: 6 to 8 servings.

SHE-CRAB SOUP WITH MARIGOLD

2 (10¾-ounce) cans cream of	¼ teaspoon garlic salt
celery soup, undiluted	¼ teaspoon white pepper
3 cups milk	1 cup crabmeat, drained and
1 cup half-and-half	flaked
½ cup butter or margarine	¼ cup dry sherry
2 hard-cooked eggs, chopped	Chopped marigold leaves
½ teaspoon Old Bay	(optional)
Seasoning	
½ teaspoon Worcestershire	
sauce	

Combine first 9 ingredients in a large Dutch oven; bring to a boil. Add crabmeat; cook over medium heat, stirring occasionally, until thoroughly heated. Stir in sherry. Sprinkle each serving with marigold leaves, if desired. Yield: 8 to 10 servings.

GEORGIA CRAB SOUP

3 tablespoons butter or margarine	1 quart milk
½ cup sliced celery	1 cup half-and-half
3 tablespoons all-purpose flour	1 pound crabmeat
	Salt and pepper to taste

Melt butter in large saucepan; add celery and sauté 5 minutes. Blend in flour. Gradually add milk and cook over low heat, stirring constantly, until slightly thickened. Add half-and-half, crabmeat, salt, and pepper; blend well. Cover and cook over very low heat for 15 minutes; stir occasionally. Yield: 6 servings.

COURT BOUILLON

¼ cup salad oil	Salt to taste
¼ cup all-purpose flour	2 bay leaves
2 large onions, chopped	1 to 2 teaspoons seafood seasoning
2 cloves garlic, minced	2 hard-cooked eggs, sliced
1 green pepper, chopped	1 lemon, sliced
4 stalks celery, chopped	Hot cooked rice
Fish Stock	
2 (16-ounce) cans whole tomatoes	
4- to 6-pound firm redfish, grouper, snapper, or catfish, filleted and cubed	

Heat oil in a heavy saucepan or Dutch oven over medium heat; add flour very slowly, stirring constantly with a wooden spoon until roux is very brown.

Add onion, garlic, green pepper, and celery to the roux; cook until vegetables are limp. Add Fish Stock and tomatoes; simmer 30 minutes. Add fish, salt, bay leaves, and seafood seasoning; simmer 20 minutes.

Just before serving, stir in egg and lemon slices. Spoon over rice in soup bowls. Yield: 8 to 10 servings.

Fish Stock:

6 cups water	1½ teaspoons salt
Backbone and head from 4- to 6-pound fish	½ teaspoon pepper
2 bay leaves	2 to 3 teaspoons seafood seasoning

Combine all ingredients in a large saucepan or Dutch oven; simmer 1 hour. Strain stock. Yield: about 5 cups.

Photograph for this recipe on page 86

HEARTY FISH SOUP

¼ cup olive oil
2 medium onions, chopped
1 medium potato, peeled and
   diced
1 cup diced celery
½ cup diced carrot
2 quarts water
1 cup dry white wine
1 (16-ounce) can whole
   tomatoes

2 tablespoons salt
Dash of pepper
2 pounds cod filets, cut into
   bite-size pieces
¼ cup all-purpose flour
½ cup uncooked regular rice
¼ cup chopped parsley

Heat oil and simmer onions, potato, celery, and carrot in kettle for 10 minutes. Add water, wine, tomatoes, salt, and pepper; simmer an additional 15 minutes.

Dredge fish in flour and add to soup with rice and parsley. Cook 20 minutes or until fish flakes and rice is tender. Yield: 10 to 12 servings.

LOBSTER BISQUE

3 cups skim milk
1 slice onion
1 stalk celery, diced
2 sprigs parsley
1 small bay leaf
1 tablespoon butter or
   margarine

2 tablespoons all-purpose flour
½ teaspoon salt
½ teaspoon seasoned salt
⅛ teaspoon pepper
1 (5-ounce) can lobster

Combine milk, onion, celery, parsley, and bay leaf in a saucepan; scald milk and strain. Melt butter; gradually stir in flour until smooth. Stir in milk, salt, seasoned salt, pepper, and lobster. Cook over low heat until thickened. Remove bay leaf and serve in bowls or in mugs to sip with main course. Yield: 4 servings.

Note: 1 (6½-ounce) can crabmeat can be substituted for lobster.

LOBSTER SOUP

¾ pound cooked lobster meat
1 teaspoon salt
⅛ teaspoon white pepper
¼ teaspoon paprika

⅛ teaspoon ground nutmeg
¼ cup melted butter
2 pints half-and-half
1 tablespoon chopped parsley

Cut lobster meat into pieces. Combine lobster, seasonings, and butter; heat. Add half-and-half and bring to boiling point, but do not boil. Sprinkle with parsley before serving. Yield: 6 servings.

QUICK LOBSTER SOUP

3 (8-ounce) packages frozen
    lobster tails, thawed
2 hard-cooked egg yolks
1 tablespoon butter, softened
1 tablespoon all-purpose flour
Grated rind of 1 lemon
Dash of pepper

1 quart milk
½ cup half-and-half
½ teaspoon salt
½ teaspoon cayenne pepper
1 teaspoon aromatic bitters
1 tablespoon dry sherry

Cut away underside membrane on lobster tails and remove meat from shell. Dice lobster meat.

Mash egg yolks to a paste; blend in butter, flour, lemon rind, and pepper. Bring milk to a boil; gradually add to egg yolk mixture, blending well.

Add lobster meat to milk mixture, and simmer over low heat for 5 minutes. Add half-and-half; bring to a boil, stirring constantly. Add salt, cayenne, aromatic bitters, and sherry. Serve hot, but do not boil after adding sherry. Yield: 6 to 8 servings.

SHERRIED LOBSTER BISQUE

2 (10¾-ounce) cans cream of mushroom soup, undiluted	1 cup half-and-half
2 (10¾-ounce) cans tomato soup, undiluted	2½ cups milk
⅔ cup dry sherry	1 (5-ounce) can lobster meat
	Sliced green onion

Combine cream of mushroom soup and tomato soup in a large saucepan; mix well. Stir in sherry, half-and-half, and milk. Drain lobster meat; remove membrane. Add lobster to soup. Bring just to boiling over medium heat, stirring occasionally. To serve, pour soup into a warm tureen or soup cups. Garnish with sliced green onion. Yield: 10 servings.

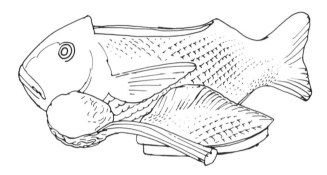

CREOLE OYSTER SOUP

2 tablespoons shortening	1 cup boiling water
¼ cup butter	¼ teaspoon ground mace
¼ cup all-purpose flour	1 pint oysters and juice
2 small onions, finely chopped	1 quart milk
1 clove garlic, minced	Salt to taste
1 stalk celery, finely chopped	Croutons, crackers, or French
⅛ teaspoon pepper	bread
1 beef bouillon cube	

In a heavy skillet melt shortening and butter over medium heat. Add flour, stirring constantly until blended. Add onion, garlic, celery, and pepper and cook for about 7 minutes. Add beef cube which has been dissolved in boiling water. Add mace and oysters with juice after checking oysters for bits of shell. Cook until oysters plump up and are ruffled around the edges. In a separate saucepan heat milk, but do not boil: add milk to oyster mixture and serve at once. If the oysters are salty, no salt need be added to the soup. Taste after milk has been added, and add salt accordingly. The oyster base may be prepared ahead of time, but be sure to refrigerate until it is used. Serve with croutons, crackers, or French bread. Yield: 6 servings.

CHARLESTON OYSTER SOUP

1 (10¾-ounce) can condensed
   cream of chicken soup,
   undiluted
1½ cups half-and-half
1 (4⅔-ounce) can whole
   oysters

½ teaspoon salt
¼ teaspoon pepper
¼ teaspoon mace

In a medium saucepan combine soup and half-and-half. Drain oysters, reserving ¼ cup liquid. Chop oysters; add with liquid to soup. Stir in salt, pepper, and mace. Heat, stirring occasionally, until very hot, but not boiling. Yield: 6 servings.

CREAM OF OYSTER SOUP

¼ cup butter
2 tablespoons all-purpose flour
1 quart milk
1 teaspoon salt
Dash of pepper

¼ teaspoon celery salt
½ pint oysters, undrained
Crackers
Toast strips

Melt butter in saucepan over low heat; blend in flour. Add milk and stir constantly until sauce boils and thickens. Add seasonings. Remove any bits of shell from oysters. Chop oysters; add with oyster liquor to hot mixture. Heat thoroughly until oysters curl. Serve piping hot with crisp crackers or buttered toast strips. Yield: 6 servings.

OYSTER AND SPINACH SOUP

½ cup finely chopped onion
2 cloves garlic, minced
   (optional)
½ cup butter
3 (12-ounce) cans oysters,
   drained and chopped
½ cup all-purpose flour

1½ quarts half-and-half or
   milk
2 cups chicken broth
2 (10-ounce) packages frozen
   spinach, thawed and pureed
1 tablespoon salt
White pepper to taste

Sauté onion and garlic in butter until tender; add oysters, and cook until edges begin to curl. Blend in flour, and cook until bubbly. Gradually add half-and-half; cook, stirring constantly, until thickened. Stir in broth and spinach; bring to a boil. Remove from heat, and season with salt and pepper. Yield: 8 to 10 servings.

SALMON BISQUE

1 tablespoon minced onion	½ cup dry white wine
6 tablespoons melted butter or margarine	1 tablespoon tomato paste
5 tablespoons all-purpose flour	1 (7¾-ounce) can pink salmon, undrained
1 bay leaf	1 cup half-and-half
1¾ cups chicken broth	Croutons (optional)

Sauté onion in butter in a saucepan about 5 minutes or until onion is transparent. Blend in flour; cook until bubbly, stirring constantly. Add bay leaf. Gradually stir in broth; cook, stirring constantly, until smooth and thick. Stir wine into sauce; cook over low heat 10 minutes, stirring occasionally. Discard bay leaf; stir in tomato paste and salmon liquid. Mash salmon, and stir into sauce.

Pour mixture into container of electric blender; blend until smooth. Return to saucepan; add half-and-half, and heat thoroughly. Serve immediately; garnish with croutons, if desired. Yield: about 4 servings.

SCALLOP BISQUE

1 pound fresh or frozen scallops	½ teaspoon dry mustard
1 (4-ounce) can mushroom stems and pieces, drained	1¼ teaspoons salt
	Dash of pepper
¼ cup melted butter or margarine	¼ cup all-purpose flour
	1 quart milk
	Paprika

Thaw frozen scallops. Remove any shell particles and wash. Grind scallops and mushrooms. Combine butter, mustard, salt, and pepper. Cook scallop mixture in seasoned butter for 3 to 4 minutes, stirring occasionally. Blend in flour. Add milk gradually and cook until thick, stirring constantly. Serve with paprika sprinkled over the top. Yield: 6 servings.

BOUILLABAISSE

3 onions, thickly sliced
3 cloves garlic, halved
1 leek, sliced
3 tablespoons olive or salad
   oil
2 (10½-ounce) cans
   condensed consommé,
   undiluted
2 teaspoons salt
¼ teaspoon pepper
Dash of cayenne pepper
1 teaspoon saffron
1 bay leaf

¾ teaspoon basil
¾ teaspoon marjoram
1 pound haddock, cut into
   2-inch squares
1 pound raw shrimp, peeled
   and deveined
1 (16-ounce) can potatoes,
   drained and halved
⅓ cup dry red wine
Chopped parsley
1 tomato, cut into wedges
French bread

Sauté onions, garlic, and leek in oil in Dutch oven about 10 minutes or until tender but not brown. Add consommé, salt, pepper, cayenne pepper, saffron, bay leaf, basil, and marjoram; cover. Heat until boiling.

Add haddock, shrimp, and potatoes; cover and simmer about 20 minutes. Add wine, parsley, and tomato. Remove bay leaf and serve with French bread. Yield: 6 servings.

SOUTHERN BOUILLABAISSE

2 pounds red snapper, mullet,
   or redfish fillets, fresh or
   frozen
1 pound raw shrimp, fresh or
   frozen
1 (12-ounce) can fresh or
   frozen oysters
1 cup coarsely chopped onion
1 clove garlic, finely chopped
½ cup butter, margarine, or
   olive oil
3 tablespoons all-purpose flour
1 cup coarsely chopped fresh
   tomatoes

2 cups fish stock or water
1 cup tomato juice
½ cup sherry
½ lemon, sliced
2 teaspoons salt
⅛ teaspoon cayenne pepper
⅛ teaspoon leaf thyme
3 whole allspice berries
1 small bay leaf
Pinch of saffron (optional)
French bread

Thaw fish if frozen. Skin fillets and cut into slices or large chunks. Thaw shrimp if frozen. Peel, devein, and wash shrimp. Thaw oysters if frozen. Set aside. Sauté onion and garlic in butter in Dutch oven until tender. Blend in flour. Add remaining ingredients except French bread; mix. Simmer gently for 30 minutes, or until flavors are well blended. Add fish, shrimp, and oysters. Simmer gently for 15 to 20 minutes, or until shrimp are tender and fish flakes easily with a fork. Serve with crusty French bread. Yield: about 8 servings.

HEARTY BOUILLABAISSE

1 leek, chopped (optional)	2 teaspoons chopped parsley
1 onion, chopped	Salt, pepper, paprika, saffron
2 cloves garlic, minced	and bay leaf
2 tomatoes, chopped	1 quart fish stock or boiling
½ cup olive oil	water
2 pounds fish, snapper,	1 cup white wine
grouper, or snook	
2 pounds shellfish, lobster,	
crab, shrimp, or scallops	

Sauté leek, onion, garlic, and tomatoes in oil. Add fish, shellfish, parsley, and seasonings. Cover all with fish stock or boiling water. Simmer for 10 minutes, adding wine during last 5 minutes. Yield: 8 servings.

FROSTY SEA BREEZE SOUP

1 (10¾-ounce) can condensed	2 tablespoons dry vermouth
tomato soup, undiluted	1 tablespoon chopped parsley
1 soup can water	4 drops hot sauce
½ cup diced cooked shrimp or	
flaked cooked crabmeat	

Blend soup and water; add remaining ingredients. Place in refrigerator for at least 4 hours; serve in chilled bowls. Yield: 2 to 3 servings.

SHRIMP BISQUE

2 pounds raw shrimp, peeled	Salt to taste
and chopped	Cayenne pepper to taste
¼ cup chopped mushrooms	2 cups chicken broth
2 tablespoons chopped onion	1½ cups half-and-half
2 tablespoons chopped celery	½ cup dry white wine
1 tablespoon chopped carrot	
3 tablespoons melted butter or	
margarine	

Sauté shrimp and vegetables in butter over low heat about 2 minutes. Stir in salt, cayenne, and chicken broth; bring to a boil, and cook 20 minutes.
   Pour shrimp mixture into container of electric blender; blend until smooth. Combine shrimp puree, half-and-half, and wine in a saucepan; heat thoroughly. Serve immediately. Yield: about 6 servings.

SHRIMP SOUP ÉLÉGANTE

1 small onion, chopped	1 (2-ounce) envelope noodle
1 stalk celery, chopped	soup mix with real chicken
2 tablespoons melted butter or	broth
margarine	1 pound shrimp, peeled
4½ cups water	¾ cup half-and-half

Sauté onion and celery in butter in medium-size saucepan until tender. Add water and bring to a boil; stir in soup mix. Add shrimp and cook 2 to 3 minutes or until tender. Add half-and-half; heat, stirring occasionally. Do not boil. Yield: 4 servings.

SHRIMP SOUP SUPREME

½ cup finely chopped celery	1 cup water
½ cup butter	¼ cup finely chopped parsley
3½ pounds shrimp	½ cup dry sherry
3 (10¾-ounce) cans cream of	¼ teaspoon hot sauce
mushroom soup, undiluted	Salt to taste
½ cup finely chopped green	Hot cooked rice
onion tops	

In large saucepan or soup kettle sauté celery in butter over very low heat for 15 minutes, stirring occasionally. Wash, peel, and devein shrimp. In separate saucepan combine mushroom soup, green onions, and water. Heat slowly over low heat; do not allow to boil. When celery is cooked, add shrimp, mushroom mixture, parsley, sherry, hot sauce, and salt. Cook over medium heat for 20 to 25 minutes until soup comes to a simmering boil. Serve with cooked rice. This will freeze. Yield: 8 servings.

SOUTHERN SHRIMP SOUP

1 small onion, chopped	1 bay leaf
1 small clove garlic, minced	Dash of thyme
1 tablespoon melted butter or	1 cup sliced okra (fresh or
margarine	frozen)
3 cups water	½ pound shrimp, peeled and
1 (2-ounce) envelope chicken	chopped
vegetable soup mix	

Sauté onion and garlic in butter in medium saucepan until tender. Add water and bring to a boil; stir in soup mix, bay leaf, and thyme. Cover and simmer 5 minutes. Add okra and simmer an additional 10 minutes. Stir in shrimp and cook for 2 to 3 minutes or until shrimp are tender. Remove bay leaf before serving. Yield: 4 servings.

stews

Hot and satisfying and full of nourishment, a stew has a way of warming you up when it's cold outside. Each of these is thick with meat and vegetables, skillfully seasoned with herbs and spices. Their flavor improves if they are made ahead—even frozen—and reheated.

Stew can be made with just about any kind of meat, with or without bones. If bone-in meat is used, ask your butcher to crack the bones. The marrow adds a marvelous flavor to the broth.

Browning the meat before adding the vegetables adds flavor and color to the stew. For an extra-flavorful broth, a few of the vegetables can be added when the meat starts simmering, such as onion, parsley, celery tops, and carrots. But most of the vegetables are added near the end; those that require the longest cooking time should be added first.

BEEF STEW

1 pound stew meat	1 large potato, diced
Salad oil	2 tablespoons dry onion soup
2 teaspoons salt, divided	mix
½ cup brown rice	3 beef bouillon cubes
2 cups boiling water	2 tablespoons all-purpose flour
8 carrots, diced	⅓ cup water

Cut stew meat into ¾- to 1-inch cubes. Brown in oil in skillet; add water just to cover and ½ teaspoon salt; cover and cook over low heat for 2 hours. Add more water if needed . When meat is tender remove from heat; separate meat from broth. Chill broth and remove surface fat.

Combine brown rice, 2 cups boiling water, and ½ teaspoon salt in a 4-quart kettle; boil slowly for 30 minutes. Add carrots, 1 teaspoon salt, and enough water to just barely cover. Cook for 20 minutes or until carrots are tender. Add potato and cook for 5 minutes.

Add soup mix and bouillon cubes which have been dissolved in boiling water or hot broth. Add meat and broth in which meat was cooked. Add water to cover and let simmer for 1 hour. Just before serving, add flour to ⅓ cup water and stir until dissolved; then add to stew. Stir until thickened and serve hot. Yield: 6 servings.

BAKED BEEF STEW

1½ pounds round steak cut	3 medium carrots, halved
into 1-inch cubes	lengthwise and cut into
2 tablespoons shortening	2-inch pieces
2 (10 ¾-ounce) cans	1½ cups commercial biscuit
condensed golden	mix
mushroom soup, undiluted	½ cup milk
½ cup water	½ cup chopped parsley
½ cup sliced onion	2 tablespoons melted butter or
¼ teaspoon savory	margarine
1 pound peas, shelled	

Brown meat in shortening; pour off drippings. Add soup, water, onion, and savory. Pour into 2-quart casserole. Cover; bake at 350° for 1 hour. Add peas and carrots. Cover; bake 1 hour longer. Meanwhile, combine biscuit mix and milk. Stir 20 times; knead on floured board 10 times. Roll into a 12- x 8-inch rectangle; sprinkle with parsley. Roll in jelly roll fashion starting at long edge. Seal ends; cut into 8 slices. Top stew with biscuits and brush with butter. Bake, uncovered, for 20 minutes or until biscuits are golden brown. Yield: 6 servings.

▪ *It's easier to cut raw meat into thin slices if it is slightly frozen. Even 30 minutes in the freezer will make slicing easier.*

▪ *When you need just a few drops of onion juice for flavor, sprinkle a little salt on a slice of onion; scrape the salted surface with a knife or spoon to obtain the juice.*

GRITS-BEEF STEW

2½ pounds beef for stew
1 cup all-purpose flour
2 tablespoons salt
½ teaspoon pepper
6 tablespoons shortening
2 cloves garlic, minced
1 quart boiling water
3 cups cooked tomatoes

1 teaspoon Worcestershire
 sauce
18 small white onions, peeled
 and quartered
7 carrots, peeled and cut into
 2-inch strips
2 cups cooked green peas
1 cup uncooked grits

Cut meat into 1½-inch cubes. Combine flour, salt, and pepper; coat meat well with this mixture. Melt shortening in Dutch oven; add meat and brown. Add garlic, boiling water, tomatoes, and Worcestershire sauce. Cover and simmer for about 2 hours or until meat is tender. Add onions and carrots, and cook an additional 20 minutes. Add more salt, if needed. Add peas and uncooked grits; cook for 15 minutes. Yield: 8 servings.

BEEF STEW WITH POTATO DUMPLINGS

2 tablespoons all-purpose flour
½ teaspoon salt
½ teaspoon pepper
1½ pounds lean beef for
 stewing, cut into 1½-inch
 cubes
2 onions, peeled and sliced
2 tablespoons bacon drippings

1 (10½-ounce) can beef
 broth, undiluted
¾ cup water
1 tablespoon vinegar
3 medium carrots, cut into
 ½-inch slices
Potato Dumplings

Combine flour, salt, and pepper; dredge meat in flour mixture. Cook meat and onion in bacon drippings until onion is tender and meat is browned. Stir in broth, water, vinegar, and carrots. Bring to a boil; cover and simmer 1½ hours or until meat is tender.

Drop Potato Dumplings on top of stew; cover and simmer 15 minutes. Yield: 4 to 6 servings.

Potato Dumplings:

1 egg, beaten
¾ cup soft breadcrumbs
1 tablespoon all-purpose flour
1 tablespoon finely chopped
 onion

½ teaspoon salt
Dash of pepper
2½ cups finely shredded
 potato
¼ cup all-purpose flour

Combine all ingredients except ¼ cup flour; form into 2-inch balls. Dredge in ¼ cup flour. Yield: 10 dumplings.

OVEN BEEF STEW

2½ pounds stew meat, cut
    into 1-inch cubes
1 (28-ounce) can whole
    tomatoes, undrained
1 cup coarsely chopped celery
4 medium carrots, sliced
3 medium potatoes, cubed
3 medium onions, chopped
1 (10-ounce) package frozen
    green peas or green beans
3 to 4 tablespoons
    quick-cooking tapioca

2 beef bouillon cubes
1 tablespoon salt
1 tablespoon sugar
Freshly ground black pepper
⅛ teaspoon ground thyme
⅛ teaspoon rosemary leaves
⅛ teaspoon ground marjoram
¼ cup red wine

Combine all ingredients in a 5-quart casserole. Cook, covered, at 250° for 5 hours. After 3½ hours of cooking, stir well; continue cooking. Yield: about 15 servings.

QUICK BEEF STEW

1 (16-ounce) can whole tomatoes	½ teaspoon basil
1 (16-ounce) can green beans	¼ teaspoon salt
1 onion, chopped	1 (16-ounce) can potatoes
1 clove garlic, minced	1 (12-ounce) can roast beef
	All-purpose flour (optional)

Drain tomatoes and beans; put juices into a saucepan and add onion, garlic, basil, and salt; bring to a boil. Add tomatoes, beans, potatoes, and meat. Cook for 10 minutes over low heat. Thicken with paste of flour and water, if desired. Yield: 6 servings.

Note: If using raw potatoes, peel 2 potatoes and cut into large cubes. Cook about 10 minutes in the vegetable juices before adding the vegetables and meat.

BEEF STEW WITH BEER

¼ cup salad oil, divided	1 teaspoon salt
2 onions, sliced	¼ teaspoon pepper
½ cup diced, pared carrot	1 (12-ounce) bottle beer
2 cloves garlic, crushed	1 teaspoon granulated beef bouillon
3 pounds chuck or round, cut into 2-inch cubes	1¼ cups water, divided
2 bay leaves	1 tablespoon all-purpose flour
¼ teaspoon leaf thyme, crumbled	1 teaspoon vinegar
	Chopped parsley

Heat 2 tablespoons oil in large kettle or Dutch oven. Sauté onions, carrot, and garlic until soft and lightly browned; remove and set aside. Heat 2 remaining tablespoons of oil in kettle; brown meat very well on all sides. This will take 10 to 15 minutes. Add onion mixture, bay leaves, thyme, salt, pepper, beer, beef bouillon, and 1 cup water. Bring to a boil; lower heat and simmer for 1¾ to 2 hours or until meat is tender. Remove bay leaves; skim off any fat. Thicken gravy with 1 tablespoon flour blended to a smooth paste with ¼ cup water and 1 teaspoon vinegar; add to stew; stir until thickened and bubbly. Remove from heat; cover and refrigerate. When ready to serve, reheat until bubbly. Sprinkle stew with parsley. Yield: 6 to 8 servings.

• *Keep bacon drippings in a covered container in the refrigerator; use for browning meats or seasoning vegetables.*

BROWN OCTOBER STEW

1½ pounds beef chuck, shank, or round, cut into large cubes
1½ pounds lamb shoulder, cut into small cubes
3 tablespoons all-purpose flour
2 teaspoons salt
½ teaspoon pepper
¼ teaspoon ground ginger
3 tablespoons olive or salad oil
1 cup chopped onion
2 cloves garlic, minced

1 quart cocktail vegetable juice
1 (1-inch) stick cinnamon
4 carrots, peeled and quartered
1 medium eggplant, cut into large cubes (do not pare)
4 stalks celery, cut into 3-inch sticks
8 large dried prunes, split and pitted
8 large dried apricot halves

Trim all fat from beef and lamb; shake cubes (a few at a time) in mixture of flour, salt, pepper, and ginger in paper bag to coat evenly. Brown quickly in oil in large heavy kettle or Dutch oven. Stir in onion, garlic, vegetable juice, and stick cinnamon. Arrange carrots, eggplant, and celery around meat. Cover and simmer for 1 hour. Stuff each prune with apricot half. Place on stew. Cover and simmer 1 hour or until meat is tender. Yield: 6 to 8 servings.

CHINESE CHUCK STEW

1 (2-pound) boneless chuck steak, cut ¾ inch thick
¼ cup all-purpose flour, divided
1½ teaspoons salt
Salad oil
¾ cup water, divided
3 onions, thinly sliced

2 green peppers, cut into strips
1 (5-ounce) can water chestnuts, sliced
2½ cups diagonally cut celery
1 (2-ounce) can mushrooms, undrained

Cut meat into 1-inch cubes. Combine 2 tablespoons flour with salt; dredge meat. Brown meat slowly in hot oil in heavy pan or Dutch oven. Add ¼ cup water; cover, and cook over low heat for 1 hour until meat is fork-tender. Add vegetables; cover and cook 10 minutes. Mix remaining flour and water; add to stew and cook until thickened. Yield: 6 servings.

CHUCKWAGON STEW

1 teaspoon sugar
¼ cup all-purpose flour
2 pounds lean beef for
    stewing, cut in 1-inch
    cubes
2 tablespoons melted
    shortening
2 teaspoons salt
¼ teaspoon pepper
1 teaspoon chili powder
¼ teaspoon thyme
1 bay leaf

2 tomatoes, peeled and
    quartered
1 (10½-ounce) can beef
    broth, undiluted
6 small potatoes, peeled and
    quartered
6 small carrots, cut into
    2-inch pieces
6 small whole onions, peeled
3 or 4 stalks celery, cut into
    2-inch pieces
1 cup frozen green peas

Combine sugar and flour. Coat beef with flour mixture, and brown in hot shortening.

Add seasonings, tomatoes, and broth to meat; cover and simmer over low heat about 1½ to 2 hours or until meat is almost tender. Stir in vegetables except peas; cover and cook about 30 minutes. Add peas; cover and cook about 15 more minutes. Yield: 6 to 8 servings.

Photograph for this recipe on page 100

CIDER STEW

2 pounds lean beef for
    stewing, cut into 1½-inch
    cubes
3 large onions, sliced
3 tablespoons bacon drippings
3 tablespoons all-purpose flour
2 teaspoons salt
¼ teaspoon pepper

¼ teaspoon thyme
1 cup apple cider
1 tablespoon catsup
3 large potatoes, peeled and
    quartered
4 medium carrots, cut into
    2-inch lengths

Brown meat and onion in bacon drippings in pressure cooker. Combine flour, salt, pepper, and thyme; stir into meat. Combine cider and catsup; add to meat, stirring until well mixed. Cover and cook at 15 pounds' pressure 18 minutes.

Allow pressure to drop to zero; remove cover, and add vegetables. Cover and cook at 15 pounds' pressure 5 minutes. Allow pressure to drop to zero before removing cover. Yield: 6 to 8 servings.

Note: Stew can also be prepared without a pressure cooker. Brown meat and onion in bacon drippings in a large Dutch oven. Combine flour, salt, pepper, and thyme; stir into meat. Combine cider and catsup; add to meat with potatoes and carrots. Cover, and simmer about 2 hours or until meat and vegetables are tender. Add water, if needed, during cooking.

COUNTRY STEW

2 pounds boneless stew meat,
  cut into 1-inch cubes
1 (17-ounce) can green peas
1 cup thinly sliced carrots
1 large potato, cubed
2 onions, sliced

1 teaspoon salt
1 (10¾-ounce) can tomato
  soup, undiluted
Dash of pepper
1⅓ cups water
1 bay leaf

Combine all ingredients in an electric slow cooker. Cover and cook on low setting 8 to 10 hours or on high setting 4 to 5 hours. Yield: 5 to 6 servings.

COWBOY STEW

1 (2-pound) chuck steak, cut
  into 1-inch cubes
⅓ cup soy sauce
1 quart water
2 teaspoons salt
1 teaspoon garlic powder
¼ teaspoon pepper
1 teaspoon Worcestershire
  sauce

4 medium potatoes, peeled
  and cubed
6 carrots, sliced
3 small onions, quartered
1 (10-ounce) package frozen
  cut green beans, thawed
½ cup all-purpose flour
¾ cup cold water

Marinate beef cubes in soy sauce for at least 1 hour, turning occasionally to coat evenly. Place meat in 12-inch skillet; add water, seasonings, and Worcestershire sauce; cover and simmer for 1 hour or until meat is almost tender. Add vegetables; cook about 20 minutes or until tender. Blend flour and water until smooth; add to mixture and bring to boil stirring constantly; cook for 1 minute. Yield: 6 to 8 servings.

HERB STEW

2 pounds beef, cubed	¾ teaspoon thyme
¼ cup all-purpose flour	¾ teaspoon rosemary
1 tablespoon salad oil	8 small onions, cut up
1 tablespoon salt	4 carrots, cut into bite-size
¼ teaspoon pepper	pieces
1 clove garlic, minced	6 medium potatoes, cut into
1 cup boiling water	bite-size pieces
1 quart tomato juice	1 (10-ounce) package frozen
2 tablespoons brown sugar	green peas
½ teaspoon marjoram	

Shake beef in paper bag with flour. Brown in oil in kettle. Add salt, pepper, garlic, water, tomato juice, sugar, and herbs (tied in small cheesecloth bag). Simmer about 1 hour or until beef is tender, stirring occasionally. Remove herbs. Add onions and carrots. Cook until vegetables are tender, about 30 minutes, stirring in potatoes and peas to cook the last 10 to 15 minutes. Yield: 10 to 12 servings.

HUNGARIAN GOULASH

2 pounds lean beef for stewing, cut into 1-inch cubes	1 tablespoon paprika
	¼ cup tomato paste
	½ cup dry red wine
2 large purple onions, thinly sliced	About 2 cups beef broth
	Salt to taste
1 medium-size green pepper, chopped	Hot cooked noodles or rice
¼ cup melted butter or margarine	

Sauté meat, onion, and green pepper in butter until vegetables are tender. Add remaining ingredients except noodles; cover and simmer over low heat 1½ to 2 hours or until meat is tender. Additional broth may be added, if necessary, during cooking. Serve over noodles or rice. Yield: 4 to 5 servings.

MOTHER'S STEW

2 to 2½ pounds very lean
  beef stew meat
2 tablespoons bacon drippings
  or shortening
2 large onions, diced
5 large potatoes, cut into
  eighths
4 or 5 large carrots, cut into
  2-inch slices

Salt and pepper to taste
Garlic powder or garlic salt
  (optional)
Diced celery (optional)
1 (10¾-ounce) can condensed
  tomato soup, undiluted
1 soup can water

Brown stew meat in bacon drippings or shortening. Add onions and cook until browned. Add vegetables and seasonings. Add soup and water. Simmer about 3 hours or until meat and vegetables are tender. Add more water as needed during cooking. Yield: 6 servings.

EASY SAUERBRATEN

1½ pounds beef, cut into
  1½-inch cubes
2 tablespoons salad oil
1 (10½-ounce) can condensed
  onion soup, undiluted
1 soup can water
¼ cup vinegar

1 medium bay leaf
⅛ teaspoon ground cloves
4 small carrots, cut into
  1-inch pieces
1 small cabbage, quartered
⅓ cup crushed gingersnaps

Brown beef in hot oil in a heavy pan; drain off drippings.

Combine soup, water, vinegar, bay leaf, and cloves; pour over beef. Simmer, covered, 1½ hours, stirring occasionally. Add carrots and cabbage; simmer 1 hour or until meat and vegetables are tender.

Remove meat and vegetables to a warm serving dish; keep warm. Slowly add crushed gingersnaps to cooking liquid, stirring constantly, until smooth and thickened. Pour over meat and vegetables. Yield: 6 servings.

SHAKESPEARE STEW

2 tablespoons salad oil (or 1 tablespoon oil and 1 tablespoon butter)	1 tablespoon all-purpose flour
	1 cup water
	½ cup dry red wine
2 onions, chopped	1 (16-ounce) can small onions, drained and well rinsed
2 pounds lean beef stew meat, cut into 1½-inch cubes	
1 teaspoon seasoning salt (or more to taste)	1 (10-ounce) package frozen green peas
Black pepper to taste	Pesto Sauce

Heat oil over moderately high heat in a large, heavy skillet. Sauté onions in oil. Before they brown, add meat, seasoning salt, and pepper, stirring constantly. When meat has lost its red color, sprinkle in flour and continue stirring and scraping until flour and meat have browned. Add water and wine, and stir in well. Pour mixture into a 3-quart casserole with a tight-fitting lid. (If lid does not fit snugly, place a piece of aluminum foil over casserole before covering.) Cook at 225° for 2½ to 3 hours or until meat is tender. If fat has collected on surface, skim off. Add onions and peas; cover and return to oven for about 10 minutes. Do not allow stew to cook until vegetables are mushy. They should remain fairly crisp, especially the peas. Just before serving, stir in several tablespoons Pesto Sauce or pass sauce separately. Yield: 6 servings.

Pesto Sauce:

2 cloves garlic	¼ cup fresh parsley, chopped
1 tablespoon pine nuts (walnuts may be substituted)	¼ cup grated Parmesan cheese
	½ teaspoon salt
1 tablespoon basil	¼ cup salad or olive oil*

Using a mortar and pestle or electric blender, grind garlic, nuts, basil, parsley, cheese, and salt. When thoroughly blended, begin adding oil, a small amount at a time, stirring to form a creamy, thick sauce. Set aside at room temperature until serving time. Yield: about ½ cup.

*You may add at least ½ cup olive oil to achieve a pouring consistency which makes pesto suitable as a sauce for pasta.

SOUTHERN HASH

4 or 5 potatoes	1 cup meat stock or gravy
2 medium onions	2 cups cooked, chopped meat
¼ cup shortening	Salt
½ cup diced tomatoes	Pepper

Put potatoes and onions through a food chopper. Melt shortening, add potatoes, onions, and tomatoes; cover pan, and cook until potatoes are done. Stir occasionally to prevent sticking. Add meat stock and chopped meat and season with salt and pepper. Heat thoroughly and serve hot. Yield: 6 servings.

STARVING CAMPERS' STEW

Salt and pepper to taste	2 cups water
2½ to 3 pounds stew meat, cut into cubes	6 medium onions
	6 carrots
All-purpose flour	2 or 3 stalks celery
Bacon drippings or salad oil	6 potatoes
1 tablespoon paprika	½ cup commercial sour cream

Salt and pepper meat and dredge it lightly with flour. Brown meat in drippings in Dutch oven. Sprinkle each piece of meat with paprika. Add water, cover, and simmer for 1 hour.

Pare and cut vegetables into chunks. Add vegetables to meat; add more water as needed, and cook, covered, until all is tender. Stir in sour cream just before serving and adjust seasonings. Yield: 6 servings.

TERIYAKI STEW

2 pounds lean stew meat, cut into 2-inch cubes	1 pound small carrots, cut into 2-inch lengths
¼ cup salad oil	4 medium potatoes, cut into quarters
Boiling water	12 whole small onions
2 bay leaves	¼ cup Worcestershire sauce
1 teaspoon monosodium glutamate	1 tablespoon cooking sherry
Salt and pepper to taste	1 pound fresh mushrooms, cut into halves
1 teaspoon bottled brown bouquet sauce or soy sauce	1 (10-ounce) package frozen green peas
1 stalk celery	3 tablespoons all-purpose flour
1 carrot	Water
1 onion	Hot cooked rice
1 bunch celery, cut into 2-inch long strips	

Brown meat in salad oil in skillet. Put into deep pot and cover with boiling water; add seasonings, stalk celery, carrot, and onion. Cook slowly until meat is tender (at least one hour).

Remove bay leaves, celery, and carrot. Add cut celery, carrots, potatoes, and small onions. Cook about 20 minutes or until onions are tender. Additional water may be added with the vegetables, if necessary. Add Worcestershire sauce, sherry, mushrooms, and peas; cook for several minutes. Mix flour with enough water to make a thin and fairly clear gravy; add to mixture and stir until thickened. Serve hot over rice. Yield: 6 to 8 servings.

TAHOMA STEW

2½ pounds chuck steak, cut
    into large cubes
All-purpose flour
Salad oil
3 onions, chopped
3 potatoes, diced
3 carrots, diced

2 stalks celery, chopped
1 (16-ounce) can whole
    tomatoes, undrained
Oregano to taste
Onion salt to taste
Garlic salt to taste

Dredge meat in flour; brown in hot oil with onion. Add remaining ingredients. Place in pressure cooker and let simmer for ½ hour on 15 pounds pressure. Thicken gravy with flour if necessary. Yield: 8 servings.

WINTER STEW

2 pounds beef stew meat
2 tablespoons shortening
1 teaspoon seasoned salt
1 cup boiling water
1 cup tomato juice

6 small onions, quartered
2 medium potatoes, diced
1½ cups canned whole kernel
    corn
1 cup sliced carrots

Brown stew meat in hot shortening in a heavy skillet. Sprinkle with seasoned salt as it cooks. Add boiling water and tomato juice; simmer, covered, for 1 to 1½ hours. Add vegetables and cook until they are tender. Add more water or tomato juice, if needed. Add more salt, if desired. Yield: 6 servings.

HUNTER'S STEW

2 pounds beef round, cubed
2 pounds lean pork, cubed
3 tablespoons salad oil
1 cup chopped onion
1 clove garlic, minced
1 (16-ounce) can whole
   tomatoes, undrainnd
1 bay leaf
½ teaspoon celery seeds

½ teaspoon caraway seeds
1½ teaspoons salt
¼ teaspoon pepper
1 medium head cabbage,
   chopped
1 (16-ounce) can sauerkraut,
   drained and washed
1 teaspoon sugar

Brown beef and pork cubes on all sides in hot oil in large kettle. Add onion and garlic; sauté until tender. Add remaining ingredients. Cover; bring to a boil; lower heat and simmer, stirring occasionally, for 1½ to 2 hours or until meat is tender. Remove bay leaf. Yield: 8 servings.

ITALIAN MEAT STEW

1 pound boneless beef, cut
   into cubes
1 pound lamb shoulder, cut
   into pieces
2 tablespoons salad oil
1 medium onion, chopped
1 clove garlic, minced
1 (28-ounce) can whole
   tomatoes
½ cup water
1 cup diced celery

2 tablespoons parsley flakes
1 teaspoon mixed Italian
   seasoning
1 teaspoon salt
½ teaspoon basil
¼ teaspoon pepper
3 large carrots, pared and cut
   into 2-inch pieces
3 medium potatoes, pared and
   quartered

Brown beef and lamb well on all sides in oil in large heavy kettle. Add onion, garlic, tomatoes, water, celery, parsley flakes, Italian seasoning, salt, basil, and pepper. Cover; simmer for 1 to 1½ hours or until meat is tender. Add remaining ingredients; simmer for 30 minutes or until vegetables are tender. Yield: 6 servings.

GROUND BEEF STEW

1 medium onion, chopped
2 tablespoons salad oil
1 pound ground beef
3 tablespoons all-purpose flour
2 cups cold water

12 small onions, partially
   cooked
Salt and pepper to taste
Mashed potatoes
Parsley

Sauté onion in oil until transparent; add meat and stir until browned. Add flour and stir until blended; add water and stir until mixed. Cover and simmer for 10 minutes. Add onions, season with salt and pepper, and cook for 10 additional minutes. Arrange a circle of mashed potatoes on a serving plate and pour meat mixture into the center. Arrange onions near edge of potato circle. Garnish with parsley. Yield: 4 to 6 servings.

CAMPSITE STEW

1 pound ground beef	3 large potatoes, pared and
½ cup chopped onion	diced
1 (10½-ounce) can condensed	1 teaspoon salt
beef broth, undiluted	Dash of pepper
1 (17-ounce) can cream-style	
corn	

Brown ground beef and onion in skillet; add beef broth, corn, potatoes, salt, and pepper; mix well. Cover; cook over low heat for 20 to 25 minutes, stirring occasionally to prevent sticking. Yield: 4 to 6 servings.

SWENSON STEW

1 (8-ounce) package wide	1 quart tomato juice
noodles	¼ cup chopped celery leaves
1 quart water	¾ teaspoon Worcestershire
2 teaspoons salt, divided	sauce
1 pound ground beef	¼ teaspoon rosemary
1 cup chopped onion	¼ teaspoon pepper
1 tablespoon butter	

Cook noodles until tender in boiling water with 1 teaspoon salt added; drain. Brown beef and onion in butter; sprinkle with remaining 1 teaspoon salt. Add to noodles along with remaining ingredients; simmer for 15 minutes. Yield: 6 servings.

KENTUCKY BURGOO

2 pounds beef shank	2 cups chopped celery
2 pounds pork shank	4 green peppers, chopped
2 pounds veal shank	4 cups chopped tomatoes
1 (3- to 6-pound) hen, cut into	2 cups whole kernel corn,
serving-size pieces	canned or fresh
2 or 3 squirrels, cut into	2 cups butterbeans or lima
serving-size pieces	beans
(optional)	2 pods red pepper
1 (3-pound) breast of lamb	2 tablespoons Worcestershire
2 gallons cold water	sauce
1½ pounds onions, chopped	Salt and pepper to taste
2 pounds potatoes, chopped	Hot sauce to taste
4 carrots, chopped	

Put meats and water into a 4-gallon kettle and bring slowly to a boil. Simmer until meat is tender enough to fall off the bones. Remove meat from stock and cool. Separate meat from bones, and chop into fairly large pieces. Return chopped meat to stock. Add onions, potatoes, carrots, celery, green peppers, tomatoes, corn, butterbeans, and red pepper to the stock. Cook until vegetables are tender and mixture is thickened. Mixture should cook slowly for several hours and be stirred often to keep it from sticking to kettle. After mixture has thickened, add Worcestershire sauce and stir well. Add salt, pepper, and hot sauce. Yield: about 50 servings.

CAESAR STEW

2 pounds boneless shoulder of lamb	3 cups diced tomatoes
1½ cups boiling water	1½ teaspoons salt
3 tablespoons onion flakes	1 teaspoon rosemary leaves
1 bay leaf	½ teaspoon freshly ground black pepper
3 pounds spinach, torn into bite-size pieces	2 tablespoons all-purpose flour
	2 tablespoons cold water

Trim excess fat from lamb and cut into 1-inch cubes. Brown on all sides in fat trimmed from lamb. Add boiling water, onion flakes, and bay leaf. Cover and cook 1 hour or until meat is tender. Add spinach, tomatoes, salt, rosemary, and pepper. Cook about 10 minutes or until spinach is done. Blend flour with water and add to stew. Cook 1 minute or only until slightly thickened. Yield: 6 servings.

CAPE TOWN BREDEE

1½ cups dried white beans	¼ teaspoon dried ground chili peppers
2 tablespoons salad oil or butter	2 tablespoons curry powder
3 onions, chopped	1 tablespoon sugar
4 pounds mutton or lamb, cut into 2-inch cubes	¼ cup water
9 tomatoes, peeled and chopped	2 tablespoons vinegar
	1 cup chopped sour apples
2 teaspoons salt	½ cup seedless raisins
	Hot cooked rice

Place beans in a saucepan with water to cover and soak overnight. Drain, cover with water again, and boil for at least 1 hour.

Heat oil in a heavy saucepan that has a tight-fitting lid. Sauté onions in oil for 5 to 10 minutes. Add meat and brown well on all sides. Add tomatoes, salt, and chili peppers. Cover and cook over very low heat for 30 minutes. Combine curry powder, sugar, water, and vinegar; stir until blended smooth. Add to meat and onion mixture and stir until all ingredients are well blended. Drain beans; add beans, apples, and raisins to meat mixture. Stir well and cover tightly. Cook over a very low heat for 2½ hours or until meat is very tender. Small amounts of water may be added if required.

When cooked according to directions, the bredee should be thick, smooth, and rich. Serve with cooked rice. Yield: 10 to 12 servings.

IRISH STEW

3 pounds boneless lamb, cubed	2 cups water
6 medium onions, peeled	2 teaspoons salt
12 small potatoes, peeled	½ teaspoon pepper

Put meat into a heavy saucepan with water to cover; add onions. Cover and simmer for 30 minutes. Drain liquid into a bowl. Skim off all fat. Pour liquid back over meat and onions. Add potatoes, water, salt, and pepper. Cover; cook until potatoes are done. Yield: 6 servings.

LEPRECHAUN STEW

1 tablespoon salad oil	4 medium potatoes, pared and cut into fourths
1½ pounds stew lamb, cut into large chunks	1 tablespoon salt
1 clove garlic, minced	⅛ teaspoon white pepper
1 quart boiling water	½ small bay leaf
3 large carrots, cut into thirds	½ cup all-purpose flour
¼ cup sliced celery	¾ cup cold water
1 medium onion, cut into eighths	Chopped parsley

Heat oil in a 4-quart heavy, covered kettle. Add lamb and garlic; cook until meat is nicely browned. Add boiling water; cover and simmer for 30 minutes. Add carrots, celery, onion, potatoes, salt, pepper, and bay leaf. Cover and simmer gently until vegetables and meat are tender, about 45 minutes. Mix flour and cold water into a smooth paste; stir into hot stew. Continue stirring until thickened. Simmer about 5 more minutes. Remove bay leaf and serve in large soup bowls garnished with chopped parsley. Yield: 4 servings.

CURRIED LAMB STEW

2 pounds lamb shank, neck, or shoulder	1½ cups 1-inch celery strips
3 tablespoons all-purpose flour	1 to 1½ teaspoons curry powder
2 tablespoons chopped onion	1 teaspoon salt
2 tablespoons salad oil	1 green pepper, cut into strips
1½ cups boiling water	3 cups hot cooked rice
1 (8-ounce) can tomato sauce	

Cut meat into 1-inch cubes; trim off excess fat. Dredge meat in flour and cook very slowly with onion in salad oil until meat is brown on all sides. Add water slowly. Add tomato sauce, celery, curry, and salt; cover and simmer for 1½ hours. Add green pepper; cover and continue cooking until vegetables and meat are tender. Serve over hot cooked rice. Yield: 6 servings.

LAMB STEW WITH PARSLEY DUMPLINGS

2 pounds boneless lamb
6 carrots, diced
3 medium onions, diced
2 stalks celery, cut into
   2-inch pieces

6 medium potatoes, quartered
Salt and pepper to taste
Parsley Dumplings

Cut lamb into 1-inch squares. Put into pan and cover with water, cover pan with tight-fitting lid, and cook slowly for 1 hour. Add carrots, onions, celery, and potatoes. Season with salt and pepper. Cover and continue cooking slowly until lamb and vegetables are done, about 1 hour. About 15 minutes before end of cooking time, bring mixture to boiling point and drop Parsley Dumplings by tablespoons on meat and vegetables. Cover tightly and cook until done. Yield: 6 servings.

Parsley Dumplings:

1 cup all-purpose flour
1½ teaspoons baking powder
½ teaspoon salt
1 tablespoon minced parsley

1 egg, beaten
⅓ cup milk
2 tablespoons melted
   margarine

Combine flour, baking powder, and salt; add parsley. Combine egg, milk, and margarine; add to dry ingredients, stirring only until flour is moistened. Drop by tablespoonfuls on meat mixture.

LAMB STEW FOR TWO

¼ pound mushrooms, sliced
¼ cup melted butter or
   margarine
1 to 1½ cups cubed cooked
   lamb
1 small onion, sliced
1¾ cups beef broth
1 teaspoon salt, divided

¼ teaspoon marjoram
Dash of pepper
2 medium potatoes, pared and
   diced
2 medium carrots, sliced
1 tablespoon all-purpose flour
¼ cup water

Sauté mushrooms in butter in a large skillet; remove with slotted spoon and set aside.

Lightly brown lamb and onion in butter remaining in skillet. Add beef broth, ½ teaspoon salt, marjoram, and pepper; simmer 5 minutes. Add remaining salt, potatoes, and carrots; simmer, covered, 15 to 20 minutes or until vegetables are tender.

Blend flour and water until smooth; stir into stew. Simmer 1 minute, stirring constantly, until smooth and thickened. Add mushrooms, and heat thoroughly. Yield: 2 servings.

HUNGARIAN LAMB STEW

1 cup dried lima beans	1 (16-ounce) can whole
3 pounds lamb or beef stew	tomatoes, undrained
meat	18 small white onions
1 teaspoon salt	1½ cups water
1 teaspoon paprika	2 tablespoons all-purpose flour
5 tablespoons salad oil	1 (8-ounce) carton commercial
2 tablespoons minced parsley	sour cream

Wash lima beans; cover with cold water and soak overnight. Or boil water and pour on beans; soak for 4 or 5 hours; drain. Cut meat into 1½-inch pieces; sprinkle with salt and paprika. Brown meat in oil turning to brown all sides. Add beans, parsley, tomatoes, onions, and water. Cover; cook slowly for 2 hours. Blend flour with small amount of cold water and add, stirring constantly. Stir in sour cream; cook 5 minutes. Serve immediately. Yield: 6 servings.

SIERRA LAMB STEW

2 pounds boneless lamb, cut	½ cup seedless raisins
into 1-inch cubes	1 (16-ounce) can whole
3 tablespoons shortening	tomatoes
1½ teaspoons salt	1 tablespoon brown sugar
¼ teaspoon pepper	½ cup grated apple
1 clove garlic, minced	⅓ cup blanched almonds,
¼ cup chopped onion	sliced or slivered
1 teaspoon curry powder	2 cups hot cooked rice
¼ teaspoon thyme	Coconut

Brown meat in shortening; pour off drippings. Add salt, pepper, garlic, onion, curry powder, thyme, raisins, and tomatoes. Cover tightly and simmer 1 hour or until meat is tender.

Stir in brown sugar, apple, and almonds. Cover and simmer an additional 10 minutes. Serve over rice, and sprinkle with coconut. Yield: 6 to 8 servings.

FRANK AND KRAUT STEW

1 large onion, sliced	3 potatoes, peeled and cubed
½ cup chopped green pepper	1 large carrot, thinly sliced
2 tablespoons salad oil	2 tablespoons brown sugar
1 (16-ounce) can sauerkraut	1 teaspoon salt
1 (16-ounce) can whole	¼ teaspoon pepper
tomatoes	1 pound frankfurters, quartered

Sauté onion and green pepper until tender in hot oil in Dutch oven. Add remaining ingredients except frankfurters. Simmer, covered, about 30 minutes or until vegetables are tender. Add frankfurters; simmer for 10 additional minutes. Yield: 5 to 6 servings.

RUTABAGA-APPLE STEW

⅓ cup all-purpose flour
1 teaspoon salt
¼ teaspoon pepper
½ teaspoon paprika
1 (2-pound) pork shoulder, cut into 1½-inch cubes
3 tablespoons salad oil
1 large onion, quartered
1 bay leaf
1 clove garlic, crushed
½ teaspoon salt

¼ teaspoon pepper
1½ cups apple juice
1 small rutabaga
3 large carrots
2 medium apples, peeled and sliced
1 cup celery, diagonally sliced
1 chicken bouillon cube dissolved in 1 cup boiling water
All-purpose flour (optional)

Combine first 4 ingredients; dredge pork in flour mixture. Brown pork well in hot oil in large skillet. Add onion, bay leaf, garlic, ½ teaspoon salt, ¼ teaspoon pepper, and apple juice. Bring to boil; reduce heat. Cover and simmer for about 1 hour or until pork is almost tender.

Peel and slice rutabaga and carrots into 1½- x ¼-inch strips; add to pan with remaining ingredients except flour. Cover and simmer for 30 minutes until vegetables and meat are tender. Thicken gravy with flour, if desired. Yield: 6 servings.

SOUTHERN STEW

1½ cups chopped onion
2 cloves garlic, minced
3 tablespoons shortening
2 pounds smoked ham, cut into ½ inch cubes
½ cup minced green pepper
½ lemon, cut into 2 wedges

½ teaspoon pepper
¼ teaspoon thyme
1 (16-ounce) can whole tomatoes, undrained
1 cup uncooked regular rice
1½ cups hot water

Sauté onion and garlic in shortening until tender. Add ham and brown lightly; pour off drippings. Add remaining ingredients. Cover tightly and simmer 25 to 30 minutes or until rice is fluffy. Yield: 10 servings.

SOUTHERN PARSNIP STEW

2 pounds pork shank or pork ribs, cut into serving-size pieces
1 quart water
1 tablespoon salt

4 cups diced parsnips
2½ cups diced potatoes
¼ teaspoon black pepper
¼ teaspoon celery salt
¼ cup snipped parsley

Place meat, water, and salt in a Dutch oven. Cover and simmer 1 to 1½ hours or until meat is tender. Add parsnips, and cook over low heat 20 minutes. Add remaining ingredients; continue cooking 20 minutes or until vegetables are tender. Yield: 6 to 8 servings.

HEARTY VEAL STEW

1½ pounds boneless veal
    shoulder, cut into 2-inch
    cubes
3 tablespoons all-purpose flour
1 teaspoon salt
⅛ teaspoon pepper
¼ teaspoon paprika
3 tablespoons salad oil or
    bacon drippings

1½ cups water
1 (10¾-ounce) can condensed
    tomato soup, undiluted
4 medium potatoes
4 medium onions
4 medium carrots
1 (16-ounce) can green peas
    or 1 (10-ounce) package
    frozen green peas, cooked

Dredge veal in flour seasoned with salt, pepper, and paprika. Brown meat slowly on all sides in oil; add water and soup. Cover and cook slowly for 1½ to 2 hours. About 30 minutes before serving, add potatoes, onions, and carrots; cover and simmer until tender. Garnish with cooked peas. Yield: 4 servings.

WHITE VEAL STEW

2 pounds boneless breast of
    veal, cut into 2-inch cubes
1 quart cold water
2 teaspoons salt
1 large onion stuck with a
    clove
1 large carrot, cut in half
1 tablespoon chopped parsley

½ teaspoon marjoram
12 small peeled onions
½ pound mushrooms, sliced
¼ cup butter, divided
2 tablespoons all-purpose flour
Juice of ½ lemon
2 egg yolks
½ cup half-and-half

Put veal into saucepan and cover with water. Add salt. Bring to a boil, reduce heat to medium, and skim off top. Add large onion, carrot, parsley, and marjoram. Cover loosely, turn heat to low, and cook for 1 hour. Cook small onions until tender in boiling, salted water. Sauté mushrooms in 2 tablespoons butter; add to onions. Set aside. Drain veal, reserving stock. To pan in which mushrooms were cooked, add remaining 2 tablespoons butter. Turn heat low and blend in flour. Add veal stock, adding water if necessary to make 1½ cups, and lemon juice. Stir. Beat egg yolks with half-and-half. Stir into stock; heat without boiling for 10 minutes. Stir frequently. Combine veal, onions, and mushrooms. Pour sauce over veal. Yield: 6 servings.

CHICKEN STEW

Salt and pepper
1 (3- to 4-pound) stewing
    chicken, cut up
½ cup shortening
3 tablespoons all-purpose flour
2 cups chopped onion
½ cup chopped celery
½ cup chopped green pepper

2 cups water
1 (4-ounce) can mushrooms,
    undrained
¼ cup chopped onion tops or
    shallots
2 tablespoons chopped parsley
Hot cooked rice

Salt and pepper chicken pieces; brown quickly in hot shortening. Remove chicken and drain on absorbent paper. Add flour to shortening, and stir until brown. Add onion, celery, and green pepper; cook slowly until tender. Return chicken to pan. Add water and mushrooms. Cover and simmer for 2½ to 3 hours. Add onion tops about 10 minutes before chicken is done. Add parsley 5 minutes before removing from heat. Serve with cooked rice. Yield: 8 servings.

EASY BRUNSWICK STEW

1 (4-pound) stewing hen
4 slices bacon, cut into 1-inch
    pieces
2 cups diced potatoes
1 (10-ounce) package frozen
    lima beans
1 (16-ounce) can whole
    tomatoes, undrained

1 medium onion, peeled and
    sliced
2 teaspoons salt
¼ teaspoon pepper
1½ teaspoons Worcestershire
    sauce
1 (10-ounce) package frozen
    whole kernel corn

Cut chicken into serving pieces; place in a large heavy kettle, cover with water, and cook until tender. Remove chicken from broth. Cool and remove meat from bones. Cut into bite-size pieces. Measure broth and, if necessary, add enough water to make 1 quart. Fry bacon until crisp. Combine broth, bacon, bacon drippings, chicken, and all remaining ingredients except corn in a large saucepan or kettle. Simmer over low heat about 1 hour. Stir occasionally. Add corn and simmer for 30 minutes. Yield: 7 to 8 servings.

BRUNSWICK STEW FOR A CROWD

3 (4- to 5-pound) hens
1 (3- to 4-pound) chuck roast
2 pounds beef liver
5 pounds potatoes, diced
12 large onions, finely
    chopped
2 gallons canned tomatoes
2 gallons canned corn
1 gallon chicken broth (See
    Index)

2 quarts milk
2 pounds butter or margarine
2 (11½-ounce) bottles chili
    sauce
Worcestershire sauce to taste
Hot sauce to taste
Salt and pepper to taste

Put hens into a large saucepan; cover with water; cook until meat is tender and falls off the bone. Remove from stock, cool, and separate meat from bones. Shred and set aside. Save stock. Cook roast in a small amount of water in a covered utensil until meat is tender. Remove from water and cut into small pieces. Boil liver in meat stock and put through food grinder. Put chicken, beef, and liver into large iron pot. Add potatoes, onions, tomatoes, corn, chicken broth, milk, and butter. Bring stew to a simmer and cook very slowly for at least 6 hours, stirring often. Add chili sauce, mix well; taste and add Worcestershire sauce, hot sauce, and salt and pepper. Yield: 40 servings.

MOUNTAIN PEOPLE'S BRUNSWICK STEW

1 (1½- to 2-pound)
  broiler-fryer chicken, cut
  into serving-size pieces
1 tablespoon salt, divided
Paprika to taste
¼ cup butter
2 medium onions, sliced
1 medium-size green pepper,
  diced
3 cups water

2 cups canned whole
  tomatoes, undrained
2 tablespoons chopped parsley
½ teaspoon hot sauce
1 teaspoon Worcestershire
  sauce
2 cups whole kernel corn
1 (10-ounce) package frozen
  lima beans, thawed
3 tablespoons all-purpose flour

Sprinkle chicken with 1 teaspoon salt and paprika. Heat butter in a large saucepan or Dutch oven; add chicken, and brown on all sides.

Add onion and green pepper to chicken; cook until onion is transparent. Add water, tomatoes, parsley, remaining salt, hot sauce, and Worcestershire sauce; bring to a boil. Cover; reduce heat, and simmer 30 minutes.

Add corn and lima beans; cook 20 minutes longer. Blend flour with a little cold water, and gradually stir into stew. Cook 10 minutes longer, stirring constantly. Yield: 4 to 6 servings.

Photograph for this recipe on page 2

POPULAR BRUNSWICK STEW

1 (4- to 5-pound) stewing
  chicken, cut into pieces
6 cups water
1 teaspoon salt
2½ cups whole kernel corn
2 cups chopped onion
2½ cups fresh or frozen
  sliced okra
3½ cups whole tomatoes
4 cups fresh or frozen lima
  beans

½ pound bacon, ham, or salt
  pork, diced
1 teaspoon hot sauce
  (optional)
¼ teaspoon pepper
¼ teaspoon thyme
3 tablespoons all-purpose flour
1 green pepper, chopped

Place chicken in large kettle; add water and salt and bring to a boil. Skim froth from surface; reduce heat and simmer about 2½ hours or until meat is ready to come off the bones. Remove chicken from broth. Remove meat from bones and return to kettle. Discard bones and skin. Skim fat from surface and reserve. Add remaining ingredients except chicken fat, flour, and green pepper. Simmer about 1 hour, stirring occasionally to prevent sticking. Combine reserved chicken fat and flour. Add to stew and stir constantly until liquid is uniformly thickened. Simmer 10 minutes to cook flour. Add green pepper. Season to taste. Serve hot. Yield: 14 to 16 servings.

TURKEY STEW

2 cups turkey broth (See Index
under Chicken Broth)
1 cup tomatoes
2½ cups whole kernel corn
2½ cups lima beans

1 medium onion, chopped
2 cups coarsely chopped
cooked turkey
¼ teaspoon ground ginger
Salt and pepper to taste

Combine all ingredients in a 3- to 4-quart kettle; heat to boiling. Reduce heat to simmering and continue cooking about 1 hour or until stew is quite thick. Stir occasionally. Season. Yield: 6 to 8 servings.

CREOLE GAME STEW

3 ducks (teal, butterball, or
mallards are best)
½ cup all-purpose flour,
divided
Salt and pepper to taste

¼ cup peanut oil
½ cup chopped onion
¾ cup chopped green pepper
3 chicken bouillon cubes
3 cups hot water

Cut ducks into serving-size pieces. Dredge with ¼ cup flour, salt, and pepper. Brown in peanut oil in a heavy skillet. Remove ducks. Add onion and green pepper and cook until onion is transparent; remove. Put ¼ cup flour into skillet and stir and cook until flour is browned. Add bouillon cubes to hot water and stir until dissolved. Add to browned flour mixture in skillet, along with ducks and vegetables. Cook over low heat for 1½ to 2 hours. Yield: 3 to 6 servings.

VENISON STEW

3 or 4 pounds venison
(shoulder or neck cuts)
¼ cup all-purpose flour
3 tablespoons bacon drippings
1½ to 2 cups hot water
1½ cups red wine
1 teaspoon mixed dried herbs
(thyme, marjoram, basil)

1 teaspoon dried parsley
1 large onion, sliced
1½ teaspoons salt
½ teaspoon pepper
4 carrots, scraped and
quartered
4 potatoes, pared and
quartered

Cut sinews and bones from venison. Cut meat into bite-size pieces; dredge in flour. Brown venison in hot bacon drippings in a large deep kettle. Add hot water, wine, herbs, parsley, onion, salt, and pepper. Cover kettle and bring mixture to a boil. Reduce heat and simmer about 2 hours. Add carrots and potatoes. Cover and simmer for 1 hour; add a little more water if needed. Yield: 8 servings.

CRAB STEW

1 dozen blue crabs, boiled
½ cup finely chopped celery
1 tablespoon finely chopped
   onion or chives
3 tablespoons butter
1 (10¾-ounce) can cream of
   mushroom soup, undiluted

1 cup milk
Salt and pepper to taste
1 to 2 teaspoons cooking
   sherry
Lemon slices

Remove meat from bodies and claws of crabs. Sauté celery and onion in butter; add crabmeat, mushroom soup, and milk. Cook over low heat for 15 to 20 minutes, stirring frequently. Season with salt and pepper.

Before serving, add sherry. Garnish with lemon slices. Yield: 4 servings.

FISH STEW

6 slices bacon
6 medium onions, chopped
2½ cups canned tomatoes,
   sieved
1 (6-ounce) can tomato paste
1 quart water
3 tablespoons butter or
   margarine

3 pounds fish
Salt
Black and red pepper
1 teaspoon Worcestershire
   sauce
1 cup catsup

Fry bacon until crisp. Remove from pan. Fry onions slowly in bacon drippings until brown. Add sieved tomatoes to tomato paste and let boil until tomatoes are thoroughly cooked (about 5 minutes). Add onions, bacon drippings, water, and butter. Boil for 10 minutes. Drop in fish which has been cut into eight pieces; season well with salt, black and red pepper, Worcestershire sauce, and catsup. Boil slowly until the fish is tender; then break bacon into small pieces and drop into stew. Yield: 6 to 8 servings.

CREOLE FISH STEW

1 cup chopped onion
½ cup chopped green pepper
¼ cup melted butter or
  margarine
1 (16-ounce) can whole
  tomatoes, chopped
1½ teaspoons garlic salt
1 teaspoon thyme

½ teaspoon red pepper
1 (10-ounce) package frozen
  succotash
2 (12-ounce) packages frozen
  cod fillets, thawed and cut
  into 3-inch pieces
½ teaspoon salt

Sauté onion and green pepper in butter about 5 minutes or until tender; stir in tomatoes with liquid, garlic salt, thyme, and red pepper. Simmer over low heat 5 minutes, stirring frequently. Add succotash, fish, and salt; cover and simmer 15 minutes or until fish flakes easily when tested with a fork. Yield: 6 servings.

LOBSTER STEW

¾ pound cooked lobster meat
1 teaspoon salt
¼ teaspoon paprika
Dash of white pepper
Dash of ground nutmeg

¼ cup melted butter or
  margarine
1 pint milk
1 pint half-and-half
Chopped parsley

Cut lobster meat into ½-inch pieces. Add seasonings and lobster meat to butter; heat. Add milk and half-and-half and bring almost to boiling point. Garnish with parsley sprinkled over the top. Yield: 6 servings.

OYSTER STEW

2 tablespoons all-purpose flour
1½ teaspoons salt
¼ teaspoon pepper
Few drops hot sauce
2 tablespoons cold water

1 pint oysters, undrained
¼ cup butter, softened
3 cups milk, scalded
1 cup half-and-half, scalded

Blend flour, salt, pepper, hot sauce, and cold water to make a smooth paste. Stir in oysters and their liquid; add butter. Simmer, stirring constantly, about 5 minutes or just until edges of oysters curl. Add milk and half-and-half; heat thoroughly. Yield: 6 to 8 servings.

Photograph for this recipe on page 5

OYSTER STEW FOR TWO

¼ cup margarine	2 cups oysters, undrained
½ teaspoon Worcestershire sauce	2 cups hot milk
Dash of celery salt	¼ teaspoon salt
½ cup diced celery	Dash of pepper
	2 tablespoons sherry

Melt margarine in a small saucepan over moderately low heat; stir in Worcestershire sauce, celery salt, celery, and oysters. Heat slowly until edges of oysters begin to curl. Add milk, and season with salt and pepper. Stir in sherry; heat thoroughly, but do not boil. Serve immediately. Yield: 2 servings.

SALMON STEW

1 quart milk	½ cup milk
½ cup butter or margarine	¼ cup all-purpose flour
1 (16-ounce) can salmon,	Salt and pepper to taste
drained, bones removed,	
and flaked	

Combine 1 quart milk and butter in a Dutch oven; place over medium heat until butter melts. Stir in salmon.

Combine ½ cup milk and flour, blending until smooth; add to salmon mixture, stirring well. Bring to a boil; lower heat. Add salt and pepper; simmer 5 minutes. Yield: 4 to 6 servings.

JAMBALAYA

2 cups diced cooked ham	½ green pepper, diced
½ pound large raw shrimp,	¼ cup diced celery
peeled	1 cup canned whole tomatoes
2 tablespoons olive oil	1 quart consommé
¼ cup minced onion	Dash of cayenne pepper
1 bay leaf	½ cup dry red wine
Salt and pepper	
1 cup uncooked brown rice	

Sauté ham and shrimp in hot olive oil; add onion, bay leaf, salt, pepper, and rice. Sauté until rice is golden colored. Add green pepper, celery, and tomatoes. Bring the consommé to a boil in a separate pan and add it to the above ingredients. Add cayenne pepper. Stir well. Cover and simmer until rice is done (about 25 minutes). Add wine and let simmer until serving time. Yield: 6 to 8 servings.

CREOLE JAMBALAYA

½ cup chopped onion	1½ pounds raw shrimp,
2 tablespoons melted butter or	peeled and deveined
margarine	1 tablespoon chopped parsley
1 clove garlic, crushed	1 bay leaf
¼ pound (¾ cup) cooked	1 teaspoon salt
ham, diced	¼ teaspoon thyme
1 (16-ounce) can whole	½ teaspoon hot sauce
tomatoes, undrained	⅛ teaspoon pepper
¾ cup canned condensed	1 cup uncooked regular rice
chicken broth, undiluted	

Sauté onion in butter in Dutch oven until soft, about 5 minutes. Add garlic and ham; sauté for 5 minutes longer. Stir in tomatoes, chicken broth, shrimp, parsley, bay leaf, salt, thyme, hot sauce, and pepper. Cover, and bring to boil. Pour into a 2-quart casserole. Sprinkle rice over top of mixture; gently press into liquid just until rice is covered (do not stir). Cover. Bake for 40 minutes or until rice is tender and liquid is absorbed. Toss gently before serving. Yield: 6 servings.

vegetable soups

Nothing sharpens appetites more on a cold, wintry day than the aromas from a bubbling pot of homemade vegetable soup. Many soups created by southern homemakers are a meal in themselves, and need only a fresh salad and crusty bread to be a hearty, nutritious meal. Hot or cold, thick or thin, vegetable soups are versatile dishes which can play an important role on every occasion.

Vegetable soups are among the easiest main dishes to prepare. They can be made from almost anything you have on hand in the kitchen, and most of them do not require hours of simmering to be good. Not only can vegetable soups be prepared well in advance of serving, but also their flavors actually improve when reheated.

When adding vegetables to homemade soup, remember that all vegetables should not be added at the same time. Vegetables that take the longest cooking time should be added first. These include green beans, potatoes (unless diced very thin), and corn. Canned vegetables need only to be heated, so add them last.

CHEESE-ASPARAGUS SOUP

1 tablespoon butter	1 teaspoon salt
1 tablespoon all-purpose flour	Dash of white pepper
2 cups milk	¾ cup shredded Cheddar
1 cup cut cooked asparagus	cheese

Melt butter; blend in flour, and cook until bubbly. Gradually add milk, stirring until well blended. Cook over low heat, stirring constantly, until smooth and thickened.

Add asparagus and seasonings. Mix well. Add cheese; stir until cheese is melted. Yield: 4 servings.

BEEF BARLEY SOUP

1 quart water	¼ cup barley
1 (1¼-ounce) envelope	1 medium carrot, thinly sliced
beef-flavor mushroom mix	

Stir water into mix in medium-size saucepan. Blend until smooth. Bring to a boil, stirring occasionally. Add barley; cover and cook over medium heat for 1¼ hours, stirring occasionally. Add carrot and cook an additional 45 minutes. Yield: 4 servings.

MUSHROOM-BARLEY SOUP

1 ounce dried mushrooms	Dash of freshly ground black
1½ cups hot water	pepper
1 small onion, minced	2 small potatoes, peeled and
2 tablespoons melted butter	diced
1 small carrot, minced	1 bay leaf
¼ cup fine barley	1 (8-ounce carton) commercial
1½ quarts chicken broth (See	sour cream
Index)	Dash of chopped dillweed
½ teaspoon salt	

Soak mushrooms in hot water for 20 to 30 minutes. Strain through fine sieve, reserving liquid. Chop mushrooms; set aside.

Sauté onion in butter in a large saucepan until soft; add mushrooms, carrot, barley, reserved mushroom liquid, chicken broth, salt, and pepper. Cover and simmer for 1½ hours. Add potatoes and bay leaf. Cover and simmer soup for 30 minutes. Discard bay leaf and stir in sour cream. Reheat soup but do not let it boil; garnish with dillweed. Yield: 8 servings.

Note: To add sour cream, stir a little of the hot soup into cream, then a little more, then stir all together. Otherwise, the cream will lump.

BEAN-BACON SOUP

2 slices bacon
1 onion, sliced
1 (16-ounce) can pork and
   beans

2½ cups tomato juice

Cook bacon until crisp; remove from pan and crumble into bits. Cook onion in bacon drippings. Add pork and beans; mash slightly with spoon or fork. Stir in tomato juice and bacon; heat. Yield: 4 servings.

CUBAN BLACK BEAN SOUP

1 pound black beans
2 quarts water
1 tablespoon salt
2 cloves garlic
1 teaspoon salt
1 teaspoon ground cumin
1 teaspoon ground oregano
¼ teaspoon dry mustard
2 onions, chopped

2 tablespoons olive oil
1 or 2 green peppers,
   chopped
1 tablespoon lemon juice
Hot cooked rice
Green onion tops or
   hard-cooked egg and lemon
   slices

Soak beans in water overnight. Next day, using same water, add 1 tablespoon salt; bring to a boil, cover, and cook until beans are almost tender. (These beans require longer cooking than other varieties.)

Crush together garlic, 1 teaspoon salt, cumin, oregano, and dry mustard. Sauté onions in oil about 5 minutes in large skillet; add green pepper and continue sautéing until onions are tender. Stir in seasoning mixture, lemon juice, and about ½ cup hot bean liquid. Cover and simmer for about 10 minutes. Add to beans and continue cooking until flavors are thoroughly blended, about 1 hour.

To thicken soup, remove 1 cup of beans and liquid and put through electric blender or fine sieve, returning puree to soup kettle. Check seasonings and correct if necessary.

Serve in bowls with mound of hot dry rice in center. Garnish top with finely diced green onion tops or with diced hard-cooked egg and thinly sliced lemon floating on surface. Yield: 6 to 8 servings.

LIMA BEAN SOUP

2 (1-pound) packages dried lima beans	¼ teaspoon pepper
1 large onion, chopped	½ teaspoon savory
1 apple, peeled, cored, and chopped	½ pound frankfurters, sliced
1 ham bone	½ teaspoon liquid smoke
2 teaspoons salt	1 tablespoon chopped parsley
	1 (16-ounce) can sauerkraut

Cover beans with water and soak several hours or overnight in large heavy pot or kettle. Add onion, apple, ham bone, salt, pepper, and savory; add enough additional water to bring level to 1 inch above beans. Simmer gently 1½ to 2 hours or until beans are mushy; remove ham bone. Put soup mixture through food mill or strainer; taste; season, if necessary. Return to soup kettle; add frankfurters and smoke flavoring; simmer gently until heated thoroughly. (If soup is thicker than desired, add milk to thin.) Sprinkle with parsley. Spoon hot sauerkraut into bowls; ladle soup over. Yield: 6 to 8 servings.

CREAMY OLD-FASHIONED BEAN SOUP

1 (16-ounce) package small navy beans	¾ cup all-purpose flour
2 pounds smoked ham hock or meaty ham bone	¾ cup minced onion
	1 clove garlic, minced
1 quart boiling water	¼ cup melted butter or margarine
¼ bay leaf	1 teaspoon salt
1 tablespoon minced parsley	1 (28-ounce) can whole tomatoes
⅛ teaspoon thyme	3 cups milk
Pepper to taste	

Sort beans, and wash thoroughly; soak according to package directions. Drain. Combine beans, ham hock, boiling water, bay leaf, parsley, thyme, and pepper in a large saucepan or Dutch oven; bring to a boil. Reduce heat; cover and simmer 2½ hours or until beans are well done. Remove from heat. Cut meat from ham hock; chop, and add to beans.

Put flour in an 8- x 8-inch pan under broiler. Broil until evenly browned, stirring frequently; set aside.

Sauté onion and garlic in butter; blend in salt and flour. Drain tomatoes, reserving juice. Gradually add tomato juice to flour mixture; cook, stirring constantly, until smooth and thick.

Add sauce and tomatoes to beans, mixing well. If too thick, more water may be added. Cover and simmer 1 hour. Stir in milk; heat thoroughly. Yield: 12 servings.

▪ *Make croutons from stale bread. Cut bread into cubes and toast at 250° until golden; then toss lightly in melted butter.*

NAVY BEAN SOUP

2 cups dried navy beans
½ cup diced salt pork
2 quarts water
2 (14½-ounce) cans stewed
  tomatoes, undrained
2 medium potatoes, peeled
  and diced

2 small onions, diced
2 carrots, diced
1 tablespoon salt
⅛ teaspoon pepper
Celery salt to taste

Sort beans, and wash thoroughly; cover with water, and soak overnight.

Drain beans, and place in a Dutch oven. Add salt pork and 2 quarts water; boil 2 minutes. Cover, lower heat, and simmer 1 hour or until beans are barely tender. Add remaining ingredients; cover and simmer until vegetables are tender, not mushy. Yield: 6 servings.

SOUTHERN BEAN SOUP

1 pound navy beans
Ham hock (smoked and meaty)
3 medium potatoes, cut into
  cubes

1 cup chopped onion
1 cup chopped celery
2 cloves garlic, minced
Salt and pepper to taste

Wash beans and soak overnight in enough water to cover. The next morning add enough water to make 5 quarts. Add ham hock and simmer for about 2 hours or until beans reach the mushy stage. Add potatoes, onion, celery, and garlic; simmer for 1 hour. Remove ham hock; add meat from bone to soup. Season with salt and pepper. Yield: 18 to 20 servings.

SOUTHERN RAILWAY BEAN SOUP

1 pound navy beans
1 ham shank
1 (16-ounce) can whole
  tomatoes
3 quarts water
¾ cup chopped onion
1 cup chopped celery

1 teaspoon marjoram
  (optional)
1 bay leaf
Salt and pepper to taste
2 cups diced potatoes
½ cup mashed cooked
  potatoes

Soak beans overnight in water to cover. Next day drain and put into deep soup kettle with all ingredients except diced and mashed potatoes. Cover and simmer at least 2 hours or until beans are tender.

Remove ham and bay leaf; skim off any fat on surface. Cut ham into small pieces and return to soup. Add diced potatoes, cover, and simmer about 1 hour longer or until potatoes are well done. Blend mashed potatoes into soup by stirring small amount of soup into potatoes, then a little more, etc., then returning all to kettle. (This prevents the soup from being watery.) Freezes well. Yield: 8 to 10 servings.

Note: This recipe may be used with a large beef bone instead of ham. A good combination is a knuckle bone plus some shank bones.

SENATE BEAN SOUP

2 pounds dried navy beans	¼ teaspoon salt
1 teaspoon salt	¼ teaspoon dillweed
1½ pounds smoked ham hock or pork shoulder	¼ teaspoon dry mustard
1 large onion, chopped	¼ teaspoon tarragon leaves
2 tablespoons butter or margarine	¼ teaspoon coarsely ground pepper

Sort beans and wash well. Place in a heavy soup kettle, and cover with water; add 1 teaspoon salt. Cover and let beans soak overnight.

Add enough water to kettle to make 4 quarts of liquid. Add ham hock, and bring to a boil. Sauté onion in butter until transparent, and add to beans. Stir in remaining ingredients; reduce heat and simmer about 4 hours or until beans are tender, stirring occasionally.

Remove ham hock from soup; separate meat from bone, and return meat to soup. Yield: 10 to 12 servings.

Note: If desired, chopped Smithfield ham may be sautéed and added to each bowl; ladle soup over ham.

MEXICAN BEAN SOUP

½ pound dry red or garbanzo
  beans
2½ pounds beef short ribs
2 tablespoons salad oil
1 quart hot water
4 large tomatoes, peeled and
  chopped

2 medium onions, finely
  chopped
2 cloves garlic, minced
1 cup finely chopped celery
½ teaspoon pepper
4 teaspoons salt
1 teaspoon chili powder

Wash beans; cover with warm water and soak overnight. Drain. Brown
short ribs in oil in kettle; cover with hot water. Add beans; cover, and
simmer for 2 hours. Add more water as needed to keep meat and beans
well covered. Remove ribs from soup mixture and cut meat from bones;
discard bones and fat and replace meat in soup. Add remaining ingredients
and cook another hour, adding water if needed. Yield: 8 to 10 servings.

MEXICAN RICE AND BEAN SOUP

1 pound pork sausage links
½ cup chopped onion
⅓ cup chopped green pepper
1 clove garlic, minced
3 cups water
2¼ cups tomato juice
1 (16-ounce) can kidney
  beans, drained

½ cup uncooked regular rice
1 teaspoon paprika
½ to 1 teaspoon chili powder
½ teaspoon salt
Dash of pepper

Cut sausage links into bite-size pieces; brown lightly in large saucepan.
Spoon off all but 2 tablespoons drippings. Add onion, green pepper, and
garlic; cook until vegetables are tender but not brown. Add water, tomato
juice, beans, rice, paprika, chili powder, salt, and pepper. Simmer, covered, for 25 to 30 minutes or until rice is tender, stirring occasionally.
Yield: 6 to 8 servings.

SPANISH BEAN SOUP

1 cup pinto beans
1 teaspoon salt
½ teaspoon pepper
2 tablespoons all-purpose flour
¼ cup butter or margarine,
  divided

¼ teaspoon saffron
1 cup whipping cream or
  half-and-half

Soak beans overnight in cold water to cover; next morning, boil 10 minutes
and skim. Add more water if needed, and cook until beans are soft. Put
beans through a food mill or sieve; return to saucepan and heat. Add salt,
pepper, and flour mixed to a paste with 2 tablespoons butter. Add saffron.
Stir until smooth; cook slowly for 15 minutes. Add remaining butter and
cream. Serve hot. Yield: 6 servings.

TURTLE BEAN SOUP

1 pound black beans	4 teaspoons salt
3 quarts water	¼ teaspoon lemon-pepper
1 ham bone with meat	marinade
½ pound lean beef, chopped	½ cup chopped parsley
2 medium onions, thinly sliced	1 bay leaf
¾ cup julienne-sliced celery	¼ cup butter or olive oil
¾ cup sliced carrots	¼ cup sherry
6 black peppercorns	1 lemon, sliced
2 cloves	2 hard-cooked eggs, sliced
⅛ teaspoon ground mace	

Cover beans with water and soak overnight. Drain and add 3 quarts fresh water to beans in a large saucepan or soup kettle. Add remaining ingredients except butter, sherry, sliced lemon, and eggs. Bring to a boil over high heat, cover, lower to a simmering boil, and cook for 3 hours or until beans are soft. Remove ham bone and bay leaf and run through a sieve or puree in blender. Reheat soup, add butter, and taste to see if more salt is needed. When ready to serve, put 1 tablespoon sherry in each soup bowl; add 1 thin slice lemon and 2 slices egg. Yield: 8 to 10 servings.

LENTIL SOUP

2 cups lentils	¼ teaspoon oregano
6 cups water	1 large clove garlic
½ pound salt pork, cubed	½ pound pepperoni cut into
1 large onion, finely diced	paper-thin slices
1 or 2 bay leaves	

Soak lentils in water for 1 hour. Fry salt pork until crisp; pour off all but 3 or 4 tablespoons of drippings. Add remaining ingredients to drippings and cook until golden brown. Bring lentils to a boil in water in which they were soaked. Add onion-pepperoni mixture and simmer for 1 to 2 hours or until lentils are tender. Remove bay leaf and serve hot. Yield: 8 servings.

LENTIL SOUP ITALIANO

½ pound lentils	1 clove garlic, minced
2 quarts water	1 (16-ounce) can whole
1 tablespoon salt	tomatoes, undrained
¼ cup olive oil	1 teaspoon parsley flakes
1 medium onion, chopped	Dash of pepper
2 stalks celery, chopped	

Combine lentils, water, and salt; cook, stirring occasionally, for 1 hour. Heat oil in small skillet and cook onion, celery, and garlic until lightly browned. Add tomatoes, parsley, and pepper; simmer 10 minutes. Stir into lentil mixture and cook 15 additional minutes or until lentils are tender. Yield: 8 to 10 servings.

BORSCH

1½ (16-ounce) cans julienne beets, undrained	2 soup cans water
1 tablespoon grated onion	3 tablespoons lemon juice
3 (10½-ounce) cans condensed beef broth, undiluted	3 tablespoons sugar
	2 eggs
	Commercial sour cream

Combine beets, onion, broth, and water in a saucepan; bring to a boil and cook over low heat for 20 minutes. Stir in lemon juice and sugar. Cook 10 minutes.

Beat eggs in a bowl; gradually add some of the hot soup, stirring steadily to prevent curdling. Return to remainder of soup. Serve hot or very cold with a dollop of sour cream. Yield: 8 to 10 servings.

COLD QUICK BORSCH

1 (16-ounce) can whole beets, undrained	¾ teaspoon salt
1 (10¾-ounce) can chicken broth, undiluted	⅛ teaspoon white pepper
	1½ teaspoons lemon juice
1 (8-ounce) carton commercial sour cream	2 tablespoons chopped chives

Drain beets, reserving liquid. Put beets through a sieve, or puree in electric blender. Combine all ingredients except chives with beet liquid; mix well. Chill. When ready to serve, sprinkle with chives. Yield: 4 servings.

EASY SUMMER BORSCH

1 (16-ounce) can beets	½ teaspoon salt
1 teaspoon minced onion	1 tablespoon lemon juice
1 (10½-ounce) can condensed beef broth, undiluted	¼ cup commercial sour cream
	4 teaspoons minced dill pickle
1 cup cold water	

Drain beets and reserve juice; dice beets and combine with juice, onion, broth, and water. Heat well; do not boil. Add salt and lemon juice. Chill; pour into soup bowls. Top each with sour cream and pickle. Yield: 4 servings.

▪ *When adding vegetables to homemade soup, remember that all vegetables should not be added at the same time. Vegetables that take the longest cooking time should be added first. These include green beans, potatoes (unless diced very thin), and corn. Canned vegetables need only to be heated, so add them last.*

BLENDER BROCCOLI SOUP

1 (10-ounce) package frozen chopped broccoli	2 beef bouillon cubes
1½ cups milk, divided	¼ teaspoon salt
1 cup half-and-half	Dash of pepper
1 teaspoon instant minced onion	Dash of ground nutmeg
	Commercial sour cream
	Snipped parsley or chives

Partially thaw broccoli; break into small chunks. Put into blender with ½ cup milk. Blend until broccoli is very fine. Add remaining milk and other ingredients except sour cream and parsley. Blend until smooth, 45 to 60 seconds. Chill thoroughly. Serve topped with a dollop of sour cream and snipped parsley or chives. Yield: 4 to 5 servings.

BROCCOLI-HAM SOUP

½ cup finely chopped ham	½ teaspoon ground nutmeg
2 cloves garlic, minced	1 quart bouillon
2 tablespoons salad oil	½ cup uncooked elbow, shell, or spiral macaroni
1 cup canned whole tomatoes	Salt and pepper to taste
1 (10-ounce) package frozen chopped broccoli or about 2 cups chopped fresh broccoli	Grated Parmesan cheese

Sauté ham and garlic in salad oil in a 2-quart saucepan until delicately browned. Add tomatoes, broccoli, nutmeg, and bouillon; simmer about 20 minutes. Add macaroni and continue cooking for 5 to 10 minutes or until macaroni is tender. Add salt and pepper. Serve in hot bowls; top with Parmesan cheese. Yield: 6 servings.

CABBAGE BORSCH

3 to 4 pounds short ribs	1 medium potato, cut into ¾-inch cubes
3 quarts water	1 medium onion, cut into ½-inch cubes
4 teaspoons salt	1 (16-ounce) can whole tomatoes
4 whole black peppercorns	1 small head cabbage
1 bay leaf	2 tablespoons lemon juice
1 to 2 bunches unpeeled beets, cut into ¾-inch cubes	1 tablespoon sugar
2 large carrots, cut into ¾-inch slices	
2 stalks celery, cut into ½-inch slices	

Combine meat, water, salt, peppercorns, and bay leaf in a large kettle; bring to a boil and simmer for 1 hour. Add beets and cook for 1 additional hour. Remove meat from broth with a slotted spoon; set aside. Add carrots, celery, potato, and onion. Drain liquid from canned tomatoes into soup; chop tomatoes and add. Cut meat from bones, discard fat and bone, and add meat to soup; simmer about 1 hour longer. About 20 minutes before serving, reheat to boiling. Cut cabbage into 1-inch wedges and remove core; add cabbage to soup and simmer about 10 minutes. Remove bay leaf. Stir in lemon juice and sugar just before serving. Yield: 12 servings.

PEASANT CABBAGE SOUP

6 beef bouillon cubes
5 cups boiling water
1 slice bacon, chopped
½ pound cooked ham, chopped
1 small head cabbage, shredded
2 onions, sliced

4 small carrots, chopped
¼ teaspoon salt
¼ teaspoon marjoram
¼ teaspoon thyme
¼ teaspoon savory
Pepper to taste
Grated Parmesan cheese

Dissolve bouillon cubes in 5 cups boiling water.

Cook bacon and ham in a large saucepan until bacon is crisp. Add bouillon, cabbage, onions, carrots, and seasonings; cover and simmer for 45 minutes. Sprinkle with Parmesan cheese before serving. Yield: 10 to 12 servings.

SLAVIC CABBAGE SOUP

2 pounds beef bones
1 medium onion, coarsely cut
3 carrots, scrubbed and sliced
2 cloves garlic, minced
2 small bay leaves
2½ to 3 pounds beef chuck, fat trimmed
1 teaspoon thyme
1 teaspoon paprika
2 quarts water

2 quarts (1 large head) shredded cabbage
2 (16-ounce) cans whole tomatoes
2½ teaspoons salt
½ teaspoon cayenne pepper
¼ cup chopped fresh parsley
Juice of 1 lemon
3 tablespoons sugar
1 (16-ounce) can sauerkraut

Place beef bones, onion, carrots, garlic, and bay leaves in open roasting pan. Add chuck, thyme, and paprika. Bake at 450°, uncovered, for 20 minutes or until meat is brown. Transfer meat and vegetables to a large soup kettle. Add water, cabbage, tomatoes, salt, and cayenne. Bring to a boil. Simmer, covered, 1½ hours. Skim off fat. (If possible, cook and refrigerate overnight at this point. Fat can then be lifted off entirely.) Add parsley, lemon juice, sugar, and sauerkraut. Simmer, uncovered, 1½ hours. Remove meat and bones from kettle. Remove meat from bones, shred, and put meat back into soup. Remove bay leaves before serving. Yield: 12 servings.

CORNED BEEF AND CABBAGE SOUP

1½ quarts corned beef broth
½ cup uncooked regular rice
1 onion, chopped

4 cups shredded cabbage
Diced corned beef (optional)

If broth is too salty add water. Add rice and onion to broth and bring to boil; cook 20 minutes. Add cabbage and cook 10 minutes or until tender. Season to taste. Add diced corned beef, if desired. Yield: 8 to 10 servings.

CARROT SOUP

1 large onion, sliced
¼ cup melted margarine
1 tablespoon all-purpose flour
4 beef bouillon cubes
1 quart hot water

4 cups diced carrots
1 cup diced celery
2 teaspoons salt
¼ teaspoon pepper

Sauté onion in margarine; add flour and blend well. Add bouillon cubes and hot water. Cook until cubes are dissolved, stirring constantly. Add carrots, celery, salt, and pepper. Simmer 2½ hours. Put through a sieve. Yield: 6 servings.

CREAM OF CARROT SOUP

1 medium onion, chopped
2 tablespoons melted butter
½ cup fine breadcrumbs
1 quart meat broth or water
1 teaspoon salt

Dash of pepper
1 tablespoon sugar
2 cups sliced carrots, cooked
1 cup evaporated milk

Sauté onion in butter for 5 minutes; add breadcrumbs, broth, salt, pepper, and sugar. Simmer 20 minutes. Add carrots and milk. Reheat and serve immediately. Yield: 6 to 8 servings.

FRESH CAULIFLOWER SOUP

1 small head cauliflower
1 quart boiling salted water
½ cup sliced fresh mushrooms
¼ cup chopped green onion
    and tops
3 tablespoons melted butter or
    margarine

3 tablespoons all-purpose flour
½ teaspoon salt
Dash of freshly ground black
    pepper
2 bouillon cubes
½ cup half-and-half
Ground nutmeg

Wash cauliflower and leave head intact with green stems and leaves. Cook, covered, in boiling salted water until just tender. Reserve 2½ cups hot broth. Separate cauliflower into flowerets. Dice cauliflower into ¼-inch pieces to make 1½ cups. Sauté mushrooms and onion in butter. Blend in flour, salt, and pepper. Dissolve bouillon cubes in hot cauliflower broth, stir into mushroom mixture; add half-and-half. Cook until slightly thickened, stirring constantly. Add cauliflower. Serve hot with nutmeg for garnish. Yield: 4 servings.

CELERY BISQUE

1 (10¾-ounce) can condensed cream of celery soup, undiluted	1¼ cups water
	¼ teaspoon ground basil
	2 tablespoons chopped pimiento
2 tablespoons commercial sour cream	Chopped green onion
1 (10½-ounce) can condensed beef broth, undiluted	

Blend cream of celery soup and sour cream in saucepan until smooth. Gradually add beef broth, water, basil, and pimiento. Heat, stirring constantly. Garnish with green onion. Serve hot or chilled. Yield: 4 servings.

CREAM OF CHEESE SOUP

2 chicken bouillon cubes	⅛ teaspoon pepper
2 cups boiling water	1 cup water
¼ cup grated carrot	1 cup evaporated milk
½ cup finely chopped celery	2 cups shredded Cheddar cheese
2 tablespoons minced onion	
3 tablespoons melted butter or margarine	1 tablespoon chopped pimiento
4½ tablespoons all-purpose flour	Chopped parsley (optional)

Dissolve bouillon cubes in 2 cups boiling water. Add carrot and celery; cover and simmer 8 minutes. Sauté onion in butter until tender; add flour and pepper, blending until smooth.

Add 1 cup water and milk to onion mixture; cook, stirring constantly, until smooth and thickened. Stir in bouillon mixture. Add cheese, stirring until melted; add pimiento. Spoon into bowls; garnish with parsley, if desired. Yield: 6 servings.

CALICO CHEESE SOUP

½ clove garlic	2 cups milk, scalded
¼ cup salad oil	2 cups chicken broth
½ cup finely chopped carrots	2 cups shredded Cheddar
½ cup finely chopped celery	cheese
2 tablespoons minced onion	2 cups medium bread cubes
¼ cup butter or margarine	¼ cup grated Parmesan
3 tablespoons all-purpose flour	cheese

Soak garlic in salad oil 2 to 3 hours; set aside. Place carrots and celery in boiling, salted water to cover; cover and cook just until crisp-tender. Drain and set aside.

Sauté onion in butter until tender. Stir in flour, milk, and chicken broth, blending well. Cook, stirring constantly, until slightly thickened. Add cheese; stir until melted. Add vegetable mixture; cook 10 minutes.

Toast bread cubes until golden brown. Remove garlic from oil. Combine oil and Parmesan cheese; toss with croutons. Serve on top of hot soup. Yield: 4 to 6 servings.

CURRIED CHEDDAR CHEESE COOLER

1 (11-ounce) can condensed	1 cup small cauliflower
Cheddar cheese soup,	flowerets
undiluted	6 cherry tomatoes, halved
½ cup commercial sour cream	2 tablespoons sliced green
¼ teaspoon curry powder	onion
1 soup can water	

Combine soup, sour cream, and curry powder; gradually stir in water. Add remaining ingredients and chill 4 hours or longer. Serve in chilled bowls. Yield: 2 to 3 servings.

FRIJOLE CHEESE SOUP

1 pound bacon
2 large onions, chopped
1 (28-ounce) can and 1
  (16-ounce) can whole
  tomatoes
1½ cups water
6 to 8 stalks celery, chopped

4 cups shredded Cheddar
  cheese
4 (16-ounce) cans pinto
  beans, pureed
1 to 2 teaspoons vinegar
Salt and pepper to taste

Cut bacon into small pieces, and fry until crisp. Drain well, reserving drippings. Sauté onion in reserved drippings until soft; drain well.

Combine bacon, onion, tomatoes, water, celery, and cheese in a large saucepan. Cook over low heat until cheese melts; stir frequently until well blended. Stir in beans and vinegar. Season with salt and pepper. Yield: about 8 servings.

HEARTY CHEESE SOUP

4 medium potatoes
1 medium onion, sliced
1 quart boiling water, divided
⅓ cup diced summer sausage
½ teaspoon thyme
½ teaspoon marjoram
1½ teaspoons salt

Pepper to taste
2 tablespoons butter
½ cup shredded sharp
  pasteurized process
  American cheese
1 tablespoon grated Parmesan
  cheese (optional)

Pare potatoes; cut in half. Cook potatoes and sliced onion in 2 cups boiling water until tender. Do not drain. Mash potatoes. Add sausage, thyme, marjoram, salt, pepper, butter, American cheese, and remaining boiling water. Simmer 10 minutes. Add Parmesan cheese just before serving. Yield: 6 servings.

PIMIENTO CHEESE SOUP

2½ cups milk, scalded
2 tablespoons butter or
  margarine
1 teaspoon cornstarch
⅛ teaspoon paprika
¼ teaspoon salt

¼ teaspoon celery salt
Dash of cayenne pepper
¼ cup chopped pimiento
2 cups shredded American
  cheese

Combine milk and butter in a saucepan; heat until butter melts. Stir in cornstarch and seasonings; add pimiento and cheese. Cook over low heat, stirring constantly, until cheese melts. Yield: about 4 servings.

COLLARD SOUP

1 bunch collard greens	1 green pepper, sliced
4 slices bacon	1 chicken bouillon cube
3 tablespoons melted butter or margarine	1 cup boiling water
	Half-and-half or milk
½ cup chopped onion	Salt and pepper to taste

Check leaves of greens carefully; remove pulpy stems and discolored spots on leaves. Wash thoroughly in several changes of warm water; drain. Cut greens crosswise in narrow strips.

Cook bacon in butter in a large saucepan; drain and crumble. Set aside.

Sauté onion and green pepper in bacon drippings 2 minutes. Dissolve bouillon in water; add to sautéed vegetables along with greens. Cover and simmer until greens are tender. Drain well.

To every 2 cups cooked greens, add 2 cups half-and-half; puree in electric blender. Add salt and pepper. Heat thoroughly, and sprinkle with bacon. Yield: 12 servings.

FRESH CORN SOUP

2 cups fresh cut corn	1 cup diced cooked chicken
1 quart chicken broth	2 teaspoons butter or margarine
½ cup cut okra (½-inch pieces)	¾ teaspoon salt
1 clove garlic, minced	½ teaspoon pepper
½ cup chopped celery	2 cups hot milk

Combine corn and chicken broth in a Dutch oven. Place over medium heat, and cook 8 to 10 minutes or until corn is tender. Add okra, garlic, celery, and chicken; simmer, uncovered, 20 to 25 minutes. Stir in butter, salt, and pepper. Gradually add milk, stirring constantly; heat thoroughly. Yield: 5 to 6 servings.

CREAM OF CORN SOUP

2 teaspoons butter	¼ teaspoon salt
2 teaspoons all-purpose flour	Dash of pepper
1½ teaspoons instant minced onion	1 cup evaporated milk
¼ teaspoon ground nutmeg	1 (8½-ounce) can whole kernel corn, undrained

Melt butter in saucepan over low heat; remove from heat. Blend in flour; add onion and seasonings. Gradually stir in milk. Cook, stirring constantly, until mixture thickens. Add corn. Heat to serving temperature. Yield: 2 servings.

CUCUMBER SOUP

1 to 1½ cups grated cucumber	1 teaspoon salt
1 quart buttermilk	Cucumber slices
2 tablespoons chopped green onion	Chopped chives

Combine grated cucumber, buttermilk, onion, and salt; mix well. Cover and chill at least 2 or 3 hours. Mix again before serving in chilled cups. Garnish with cucumber slices and chives. Yield: 6 to 8 servings.

Note: Scoop out and discard seeds before grating cucumber.

CREAMY LETTUCE SOUP

1 head iceberg lettuce
2 chicken bouillon cubes,
  crumbled
¾ cup water
2 tablespoons lemon juice
½ cup onion, sliced in rings
¼ cup butter or margarine
¼ cup all-purpose flour

½ teaspoon salt
¼ teaspoon white pepper
Dash of ground nutmeg
2 cups milk
¼ cup white wine
Additional shredded lettuce
  (optional)

Core, rinse, and drain lettuce thoroughly; shred enough to measure 4 cups when packed. Put lettuce, bouillon cubes, water, and lemon juice into blender; blend until smooth.

Sauté onion in butter in a saucepan until tender but not brown; using a slotted spoon, remove onion from pan.

Blend flour, salt, pepper, and nutmeg with butter in pan; stir in milk. Cook, stirring constantly, until mixture comes to a boil and is thick. Blend in wine and pureed lettuce mixture. Add onion; heat thoroughly.

Serve immediately with additional crisp shredded lettuce in center, if desired. Yield: 6 servings.

TURNIP GREEN SOUP

1 pound ham hocks	¾ pound pepperoni, thinly
1 quart water	sliced
2 to 3 pounds fresh turnip	2 (15-ounce) cans Great
greens	Northern beans, undrained
4 slices bacon	

Boil ham hocks in water about 1 hour or until ham is done. Remove meat from bones, and cut into chunks. Wash greens thoroughly in several changes of warm water; set aside. Cook bacon until crisp; drain and crumble, reserving drippings.

Return ham chunks to boiling water; add greens, bacon, reserved drippings, pepperoni, and beans. Cover and simmer 1 hour, stirring occasionally. Yield: 6 to 8 servings.

Note: Two 15-ounce cans turnip greens or three 10-ounce packages frozen turnip greens may be substituted for fresh greens.

FRESH MUSHROOM BISQUE

2 tablespoons melted butter or	1½ cups milk, scalded and
margarine	divided
3 tablespoons all-purpose flour	½ cup sliced mushrooms
¾ teaspoon salt	½ cup chopped mushrooms
Dash of white pepper	½ teaspoon minced onion
1⅓ cups half-and-half,	2 teaspoons melted butter or
scalded	margarine
⅓ cup chicken broth, heated	

Combine 2 tablespoons melted butter, flour, salt, and pepper in a heavy saucepan; blend well. Simmer 2 minutes. Combine half-and-half, broth, and 1¼ cups milk; gradually add to flour mixture, stirring constantly, until smooth. Cook over medium heat until thickened. Remove from heat, and set aside.

Sauté mushrooms and onion in 2 teaspoons melted butter 6 to 8 minutes, stirring frequently. Add remaining ¼ cup milk; heat to simmering. Stir into milk mixture; heat thoroughly. Serve immediately. Yield: about 4 servings.

FRESH MUSHROOM SOUP

1 pound fresh mushrooms	1 quart water
6 tablespoons melted butter or margarine, divided	3 tablespoons tomato paste
2 cups chopped celery	4 sprigs parsley
2 cups chopped carrots	4 celery leaves
1 cup chopped onion	¼ teaspoon salt
1 clove garlic, minced	⅛ teaspoon pepper
2 (10½-ounce) cans beef broth, undiluted	1 bay leaf

Slice 6 large mushrooms in half lengthwise; set aside. Finely chop remaining mushrooms; sauté in 4 tablespoons butter 3 minutes in a Dutch oven. Add celery, carrots, onion, and garlic; sauté 5 minutes.

Stir remaining ingredients into sautéed vegetables. Bring to a boil; cover and simmer 1 hour. Cool to lukewarm, and remove bay leaf. Process soup, 2 cups at a time, at high speed of electric blender; return to Dutch oven.

Sauté sliced mushrooms in 2 tablespoons butter 5 minutes; stir into soup, and heat thoroughly. Yield: about 6 to 8 servings.

CHILLED CURRIED MUSHROOM SOUP

1 pound fresh mushrooms	¼ teaspoon salt
5 tablespoons butter or margarine, divided	⅛ teaspoon white pepper
1 teaspoon curry powder	3 cups milk or half-and-half
2 tablespoons all-purpose flour	Commercial sour cream
1 (10½-ounce) can condensed beef broth, undiluted	Dash of curry powder

Rinse, pat dry, and dice mushrooms (makes about 5 cups). Heat 4 tablespoons butter in a large saucepan; add curry powder, then mushrooms; sauté over high heat until lightly browned, stirring constantly. Remove mushrooms and set aside. In same saucepan, heat remaining tablespoon butter; stir in flour. Add broth, salt, and pepper. Cook until thickened, stirring often; add milk. Cook 8 minutes longer. Do not boil. Return sautéed mushrooms to soup. Chill. Serve in mugs; garnish with a dollop of sour cream and a dash of curry powder. Yield: 5 to 6 servings.

CONSOMMÉ AUX CHAMPIGNONS

½ cup sliced mushrooms	1⅓ cups water
2 teaspoons melted butter	¼ cup sliced ripe olives
1 (10½-ounce) can consommé	Dash of sherry

Sauté mushrooms in butter; stir in consommé, water, and olives. Heat thoroughly. Just before serving, add sherry. Yield: 4 servings.

OKRA SOUP

1 meaty ham bone
3 quarts water
2 large onions, chopped
3 pounds okra, cut into
 ¼-inch slices
8 large tomatoes, peeled and
 cubed

2 tablespoons Worcestershire
 sauce
1 bay leaf
1 teaspoon ground thyme
Salt and pepper to taste

Simmer ham bone in water 2 hours. Add remaining ingredients, and simmer 2 hours; remove bay leaf. Cool; then cover and refrigerate 2 days. Heat and serve. Yield: 12 to 14 servings.

ONION SOUP

1½ cups butter
4 cups sliced white onion
1¾ cups all-purpose flour
3 quarts beef broth (See
 Index)
1½ tablespoons salt
½ teaspoon cayenne pepper

1 egg yolk
2 tablespoons half-and-half
Croutons or toasted bread
 rounds
Parmesan cheese
Buttered breadcrumbs

Melt butter in a 6-quart kettle. Add onion, reduce heat to very low, and cook until clear and transparent; be careful not to brown the onion in the first stages of cooking. Add flour and cook 5 to 10 minutes longer, stirring occasionally. Blend in beef broth, salt, and cayenne and bring to a boil. Reduce heat and simmer about 15 minutes. Remove kettle from heat.

Beat egg yolk and cream together; add a little of the soup and mix quickly; then add to the soup kettle. Serve in soup cups with croutons. Sprinkle with Parmesan cheese and buttered breadcrumbs. Brown under broiler, and serve hot. Yield: 12 to 15 servings.

FRENCH ONION SOUP

2 (10½-ounce) cans
 condensed beef broth,
 undiluted
7½ cups water
3 (1⅜-ounce) envelopes dry
 onion-soup mix

½ teaspoon salt
10 to 12 slices French bread
¼ cup grated Parmesan
 cheese
⅔ cup claret or dry red wine

Combine broth and water in large kettle; bring to boil over high heat. Stir in onion-soup mix and salt; reduce heat; cover, and simmer for 15 minutes.

Toast bread slices in broiler, turning to brown both sides. Sprinkle one side of each slice with Parmesan; broil about 1 minute, or until cheese is bubbly. Remove soup from heat; stir in wine. Pour soup into warm bowls. Float toast, cheese side up, on top. Yield: 10 to 12 servings.

FRENCH ONION SOUP AU GRATIN

2 medium onions, very thinly
   sliced
2 tablespoons melted butter or
   margarine
1 quart beef broth
½ cup water

Salt and pepper to taste
½ cup Madeira wine
   (optional)
Parmesan croutons
½ cup shredded Swiss cheese

Cook onions in butter in large skillet, covered, until onions are tender
(about 5 minutes). Uncover skillet, and continue cooking onions until well
browned; stir occasionally. Stir in broth and water; cover and simmer 30
minutes. Add salt and pepper; stir in wine, if desired.

Ladle soup into individual ovenproof dishes; place a Parmesan crouton
on each serving, and sprinkle with Swiss cheese. Bake at 400° for 15
minutes or until cheese is melted and golden brown. Yield: 4 to 6 servings.

Parmesan Croutons:

2 to 3 (1-inch-thick) slices
   French bread, cut in half
¼ cup melted butter or
   margarine

¼ cup grated Parmesan
   cheese

Brush both sides of bread with butter; sprinkle with Parmesan cheese.
Place on a cookie sheet, and bake at 350° for 20 minutes or until crisp and
brown. Yield: 4 to 6 large croutons.

QUICK ONION SOUP

6 medium onions, thinly sliced
½ cup melted butter or
    margarine
1 teaspoon sugar
3 dashes of ground nutmeg
8 rounded teaspoons beef
    stock base

7 cups boiling water
¼ to ½ cup cooking sherry
Salt
Big croutons
Grated Parmesan cheese

Sauté sliced onions in melted butter with sugar and nutmeg. Cook just until onions are transparent, but not browned. Dissolve beef stock base in boiling water in a large saucepan. Add onions and simmer for about 20 minutes. Add sherry during the last 2 minutes of cooking. Taste, and add salt if needed. Spoon into serving dishes; add croutons and top with grated Parmesan cheese. Put under broiler for about 10 minutes. Yield: about 6 to 8 servings.

FRENCH ONION SOUP ESCOFFIER

½ cup butter	1 bay leaf
2½ pounds onions, sliced	1½ teaspoons celery salt
1 quart beef broth (See Index)	1 teaspoon black pepper or
1 quart chicken broth (See	12 peppercorns, crushed
Index)	Salt to taste
2 tablespoons Worcestershire	French garlic croutons
sauce	1 cup grated Parmesan cheese

Heat butter in a heavy kettle. Add sliced onions and brown well, stirring constantly. Add beef and chicken broths, Worcestershire sauce, bay leaf, celery salt, pepper, and salt. Allow to simmer 40 minutes. Remove bay leaf. Serve soup at once in heated tureen; float croutons and sprinkle cheese on top. Yield: 10 to 12 servings.

SHERRIED ONION SOUP

9 to 10 onions, thinly sliced	Chicken Stock
2 tablespoons melted butter	¼ cup dry sherry
1 tablespoon olive oil	Salt to taste
1 heaping tablespoon	Croutons
all-purpose flour	Grated Parmesan cheese
½ teaspoon prepared mustard	

Slowly stir onions in butter and olive oil over medium to low heat until they are browned. This will take about an hour. (Hint: You may need to put the pan in cold water from time to time to cool the butter in order not to cook onions too brown.)

When onions are browned to color of hazelnuts, add flour, mustard, and chicken stock. (Add water if soup is too thick.) Add dry sherry and salt. Serve hot with croutons and grated Parmesan cheese. This soup can be made ahead of time and frozen. Yield: 6 to 8 servings.

Chicken Stock:

Chicken necks and backs	1 carrot, sliced
½ bay leaf	1 large stalk celery, chopped
1 whole clove	Parsley
1 onion, chopped	½ cup dry vermouth

Put ingredients into a 4-quart kettle and fill with water. Cook for about 2 hours. Strain through cheesecloth.

• *Don't throw away cheese that has dried out or any small leftover pieces. Grate the cheese; cover and refrigerate for use in casseroles or other dishes.*

ONION SOUP WITH PUFFY CHEESE CROUTONS

4 cups thinly sliced onion
¼ cup melted butter
2 tablespoons all-purpose flour
2 (10½-ounce) cans
    condensed beef broth,
    undiluted

1 (10¾-ounce) can condensed
    chicken broth, undiluted
1 soup can water
Puffy Cheese Croutons

Sauté onion in butter until limp but not brown; blend in flour. Add broth and water; stir until smooth. Simmer about 30 minutes. Serve soup with Puffy Cheese Croutons. Yield: 6 to 8 servings.

Puffy Cheese Croutons:

¼ cup butter
1 tablespoon milk
1 cup shredded Cheddar
    cheese

2 egg whites
French bread

Melt butter in top of double boiler over hot, but not boiling, water or in a saucepan over very low heat. Add milk and cheese, stirring constantly until cheese is melted. Remove from heat.

    Beat eggs whites until stiff but not dry; gently fold into cheese mixture. Cut 30 bite-size cubes of French bread; dip into egg-cheese mixture. Bake on ungreased cookie sheet at 400° for 10 to 15 minutes or until lightly browned. Remove immediately. Yield: 30 croutons.

SPRING ONION SOUP

¼ cup butter
⅔ cup thinly sliced green
　onions and tops
½ cup finely diced celery
¼ cup all-purpose flour
1½ teaspoons salt
Dash of pepper

1 quart milk
1 cup chicken broth (See
　Index)
½ cup shredded sharp
　pasteurized process
　American cheese
Toast squares

Melt butter in large saucepan; add onion and celery; cook until tender, but not brown. Blend in flour, salt, and pepper. Gradually stir in milk and chicken broth. Cook until thickened, stirring constantly. Stir in cheese. Pour soup into heated bowls and top with toast squares. Yield: 6 servings.

CREAMY BLACK-EYED PEA SOUP

1 cup dried black-eyed peas
2 quarts water
1 clove garlic, minced
1 large onion, sliced
½ bay leaf
2 teaspoons salt

¼ teaspoon pepper
1 cup diced cooked carrot
1 quart milk
¾ pound bulk pork sausage
Chopped parsley

Wash peas and soak in water for 2 hours. Add garlic, onion, and bay leaf; simmer 1½ hours or until peas are tender. Add salt and pepper. Mash peas with potato masher; add carrot and milk. Shape sausage into tiny balls and fry slowly until well done. Sprinkle soup with parsley and add sausage balls. Yield: 10 to 12 servings.

SPLIT PEA SOUP

2 cups split peas
18 cups water, divided
Ham bone or 2-inch cube of
　salt pork
½ cup chopped onion
1 cup chopped celery

½ cup chopped carrot
2 cups milk
2 tablespoons butter
2 tablespoons all-purpose flour
Salt to taste

Soak peas for 12 hours in 6 cups water; drain the peas and put into a large kettle. Add remaining 12 cups water and ham bone or salt pork and simmer, covered, for 3 hours. Add onion, celery, and carrot; simmer 1 hour longer. Put soup through a food mill or process in blender. Chill and remove all fat. Add milk.

　Melt butter; stir in flour until mixture is smooth. Add to soup stock and stir until it boils. Taste and add salt. Yield: 12 servings.

SPLIT PEA AND FRANKFURTER SOUP

1 cup split peas	3 frankfurters, cut into ¼-inch
1 quart water	slices
1½ teaspoons salt	2 tablespoons melted butter or
1 small onion, sliced	margarine
½ cup chopped celery	Croutons (optional)

Sort peas, and wash thoroughly; set peas aside.

Combine water and salt in a large Dutch oven; bring to a boil. Add peas, and allow water to return to a boil. Cover and cook over low heat 1 hour, stirring often. Add onion and celery, and continue cooking over low heat 30 minutes, stirring often.

Sauté frankfurter slices in butter until lightly browned; set aside.

Place pea mixture in container of electric blender, and process until smooth. Return pea mixture to Dutch oven. Add frankfurter slices, and simmer 10 to 15 minutes, stirring often. Serve with croutons, if desired. Yield: 4 servings.

CHILLED SPLIT PEA SOUP

1 (12-ounce) can vegetable	¼ cup finely chopped green
juice cocktail	pepper
1 (11½-ounce) can condensed	1 teaspoon salt
split pea soup, undiluted	1 slice bacon, cooked crisp
1 stalk celery, finely chopped	and crumbled
1 small carrot, finely chopped	

Combine vegetable juice cocktail, pea soup, celery, carrot, green pepper, and salt; bring to a boil, then simmer 10 minutes. Cool. Cover and chill. Serve cold with bacon sprinkled on top. Yield: 4 to 5 servings.

ITALIAN SPLIT PEA SOUP

1 (16-ounce) package dried	1 small head cabbage, cut
split peas	into 1-inch cubes
5 quarts water	¾ cup olive oil
Salt to taste	2 small cloves garlic, crushed
1 (16-ounce) can peas,	½ teaspoon cayenne pepper
undrained	
1 head cauliflower, separated	
into flowerets	

Wash dried peas; cook in boiling salted water until soft.

Mash a small amount of cooked peas into a fine paste to thicken cooking liquid; add to remaining cooked peas along with canned peas, cauliflower, cabbage, olive oil, garlic, and cayenne. Simmer over low heat 1½ to 2 hours or until vegetables are tender. Yield: about 12 servings.

PEA SOUP ELEGANTE

2 teaspoons instant beef
  bouillon
1 cup hot water
2 (17-ounce) cans small early
  peas, undrained
1 (8-ounce) carton commercial
  sour cream

½ teaspoon onion salt
½ teaspoon salt
Dash of pepper
Paprika

Dissolve bouillon in water; set aside.

Place peas in container of electric blender; blend until smooth. Add bouillon; blend well. Pour half of mixture into a large bowl. Add sour cream, onion salt, salt, and pepper to mixture in blender; blend until smooth. Stir into mixture in bowl; chill for 1 to 2 hours. Sprinkle each serving with paprika. Yield: about 6 cups.

OLD-FASHIONED SPLIT PEA SOUP

1 pound green split peas
2½ quarts water
1 meaty ham bone
1½ cups sliced onion
½ teaspoon pepper
¼ teaspoon garlic salt

¼ teaspoon marjoram
1 cup diced celery
1 cup sliced carrot
1 teaspoon parsley flakes
Salt to taste

Cover peas with water and soak overnight. Drain. Add 2½ quarts water, ham bone, onion, pepper, garlic salt, and marjoram. Bring to a boil, cover, and simmer 2 hours. Stir occasionally. Remove bone; cut off any bits of meat. Return meat to soup; add remaining ingredients. Cook slowly for 45 minutes. Yield: 8 to 10 servings.

EASY POTATO SOUP

4 slices bacon
1 teaspoon butter
¼ cup minced onion
1 (10¾-ounce) can condensed
  cream of potato soup,
  undiluted

½ soup can milk
½ soup can water
Cayenne pepper
Salt to taste
Paprika

Cook bacon until crisp. Drain. Pour off half of the bacon drippings and add butter. Sauté onion in the drippings until tender and golden. Combine soup, milk, and water in a saucepan; add a sprinkle of cayenne pepper and salt. Heat, stirring frequently. Crumble bacon and add to soup along with onion. Continue heating and stirring. Garnish with paprika. Yield: 3 to 4 servings.

HEARTY POTATO SOUP

6 medium potatoes	⅓ cup all-purpose flour
1 teaspoon salt	½ pound ground beef
2 slices bacon	1 quart milk
1 small onion, chopped	Salt and pepper to taste

Peel and dice potatoes; cover with water, add salt, and cook until tender. Mash slightly. Cut bacon into small pieces, mix with onion, and sauté until bacon is crisp and onion is clear. Remove onion and bacon from drippings and add to cooked potatoes. Work flour into ground meat until it is in coarse crumbles; fry in bacon drippings until crisp. Add to potatoes. Stir in milk and season with salt and pepper. Heat just to boiling point but do not boil. Yield: 8 to 10 servings.

POTATO SOUP FOR TWO

2 medium potatoes, finely chopped	2 cups milk
1 tablespoon chopped onion	2 tablespoons butter, softened
1 tablespoon chopped celery	Salt and pepper to taste
	Chopped parsley

Barely cover potatoes, onion, and celery with water and cook until tender. Mash with potato masher. Add milk, butter, salt, and pepper. Serve topped with chopped parsley. Yield: 2 servings.

BAVARIAN POTATO SOUP

½ cup butter	4 cups diced potato
1 carrot, diced	Salt and white pepper to taste
1 leek, diced (optional)	Dash of ground nutmeg
4 medium onions, diced	Bouquet garni
½ cup diced celery	1 cup half-and-half or
2 cloves garlic, minced	evaporated milk
2 bay leaves	
2 to 3 quarts chicken broth (See Index)	

Melt butter in heavy soup kettle; add carrot, leek, onions, celery, and garlic. Sauté about 5 minutes; do not allow vegetables to brown. Add bay leaves and chicken broth; simmer 10 to 15 minutes partially covered. Add potato, salt, pepper, nutmeg, and bouquet garni. Cover and simmer until potato is tender. Just before serving remove bouquet garni and bay leaves and stir in half-and-half. Yield: 8 to 10 servings.

POTATO-CELERY SOUP

6 medium potatoes, peeled and cut into ½-inch cubes	Salt to taste
	Dash of pepper
1 cup diced celery	2½ cups milk
½ cup chopped onion	5 tablespoons butter
2 cups water	Chopped parsley (optional)
3 chicken bouillon cubes	

Combine potatoes, celery, onion, water, bouillon cubes, salt, and pepper in saucepan; cook over medium heat until vegetables are tender, about 15 minutes. (Most of the liquid will be absorbed.) Add milk and butter; heat thoroughly. Serve immediately. Garnish with chopped parsley, if desired. Yield: 5 to 6 servings.

POTATO-FRANKS SOUP FOR TWO

1 medium onion, finely chopped	1½ cups diced potato
	3 cups water
1 small carrot, chopped	1 teaspoon salt
1 stalk celery, chopped	Dash of pepper
3 tablespoons melted butter or margarine	4 cooked frankfurters, sliced
	Chopped parsley

Sauté onion, carrot, and celery in butter about 10 minutes. Add potato, water, salt, and pepper; bring to a boil. Cover, and simmer 45 minutes. Add frankfurters; heat thoroughly. Sprinkle with parsley before serving. Yield: 2 to 3 servings.

RUTABAGA AND POTATO SOUP

1 small rutabaga	2 cups milk
1½ cups water	¾ teaspoon sugar
1 teaspoon salt	2 tablespoons butter or margarine
3 medium potatoes, thinly sliced	Dash of white pepper

Peel and cut rutabaga into small chips; add salted water and cook about 15 to 20 minutes. Add sliced potatoes and continue cooking about 10 minutes or until tender. Do not drain. Mash thoroughly; add milk, sugar, butter, pepper, and additional salt, if needed. Reheat and serve hot. Yield: 4 servings.

▪ *Stains or discolorations on aluminum utensils can be removed by boiling a solution of 2 to 3 tablespoons cream of tartar, lemon juice, or vinegar to each quart of water in the utensil for 5 to 10 minutes.*

SOUR CREAM-POTATO SOUP

4 medium potatoes, pared and
    cut into small pieces
1 medium onion, chopped
1 cup chopped celery
3 cups water
1 teaspoon salt
¼ teaspoon pepper

3 cups milk, divided
1 tablespoon all-purpose flour
1 (8-ounce) carton commercial
    sour cream
2 tablespoons butter
¼ cup minced parsley

Cook potatoes, onion, and celery in water until tender; put through food mill. Add seasonings and 2½ cups milk. Blend flour with remaining ½ cup milk until smooth; add to potato mixture and bring to boiling point. Cook about 5 minutes. Blend in sour cream and butter; heat thoroughly. Add parsley and serve immediately. Yield: 6 servings.

PUMPKIN SOUP

1 large onion, chopped
¼ cup butter or margarine
½ teaspoon curry powder
1 (16-ounce) can mashed
    pumpkin
1½ teaspoons salt

2 cups half-and-half
2½ cups chicken broth
Chopped parsley, commercial
    sour cream, or ground
    cinnamon (optional)

Sauté onion in butter until tender; sprinkle with curry powder, and sauté an additional 2 minutes. Stir in pumpkin and salt; add half-and-half, stirring constantly. Stir in broth, and heat thoroughly. If desired, garnish with parlsey, sour cream, or ground cinnamon. Yield: 8 servings.

SPINACH SOUP WITH SHRIMP

2 tablespoons butter
1 tablespoon grated onion
3 tablespoons all-purpose flour
2 cups half-and-half
3 cups cooked spinach
1 cup beef broth (See Index)

Salt and pepper to taste
¼ cup coarsely chopped
    cooked shrimp
½ cup sherry
1½ cups chopped toasted
    almonds

Melt butter in a heavy 2½-quart saucepan; stir in onion and flour. Cook slowly for 2 minutes without browning. Bring half-and-half to a simmer in another pan. Remove onion mixture from heat and beat in half-and-half, blending thoroughly. Puree spinach with beef broth in an electric blender; add to mixture in saucepan. Simmer 10 minutes, stirring constantly. Season. If necessary, thin with more half-and-half or beef broth. Keep over simmering water, stirring occasionally, until 5 minutes before serving time. Then stir in shrimp and sherry; simmer about ½ minute. Serve in soup bowls; sprinkle almonds on top. Yield: 6 servings.

GOLDEN SQUASH SOUP

1 medium onion, finely chopped	1 cup milk
¼ cup butter or margarine	1½ cups cooked yellow squash
2 tablespoons all-purpose flour	2 teaspoons Worcestershire sauce
¾ teaspoon salt	1 egg yolk, slightly beaten
Dash of pepper	½ cup half-and-half
⅓ teaspoon ground nutmeg	Croutons
1¾ cups chicken broth (See Index)	

Sauté onion in butter until soft, about 5 minutes. Add flour, salt, pepper, and nutmeg and stir until blended and bubbly. Remove from heat and gradually stir in chicken broth and milk. Return to heat, bring to a boil, and cook, stirring, until thickened. Add squash and Worcestershire sauce, reduce heat to low, and cook, stirring often, until heated thoroughly.

Combine egg yolk and half-and-half; stir in some of hot soup, then stir egg mixture back into the remaining hot soup. Cook until soup is thoroughly heated and the egg has thickened. Serve in heated bowls and garnish with croutons. Yield: 6 servings.

ZUCCHINI SOUP

2 pounds ground chuck	1 teaspoon Italian seasoning
2 cups celery, cut into ½-inch slices	1 teaspoon oregano leaves
2 pounds zucchini, cut into ½-inch slices	1 teaspoon sugar
1 cup chopped onion	½ teaspoon basil leaves
2 (28-ounce) cans whole tomatoes, cut into quarters	2 green peppers, cut into ½-inch squares
2 teaspoons salt	Grated Parmesan cheese (optional)

Brown meat in a large Dutch oven; drain well. Add celery; cook over medium heat 10 minutes. Add zucchini, onion, tomatoes, and seasonings; cook over low heat 30 minutes. Add green pepper; cover and simmer 10 minutes. Sprinkle with Parmesan cheese, if desired. Yield: 10 to 12 servings.

Photograph for this recipe on page 163

TOMATO SOUP WITH HERBS

1 (10¾-ounce) can condensed tomato soup, undiluted	4 whole cloves
½ bay leaf	½ teaspoon celery seeds
	¼ teaspoon marjoram

Prepare soup according to label directions. Add remaining ingredients and heat to boiling. Simmer 5 minutes. Strain before serving. Yield: 4 servings.

ITALIAN TOMATO SOUP

3 cups water
1 (2-ounce) envelope country
   vegetable beef soup with
   noodles
1 (20-ounce) can garbanzo
   beans (chick-peas), drained

1 cup canned Italian tomatoes
Dash of oregano
Grated Parmesan cheese

In medium-size saucepan, stir water into soup mix and bring to a boil.
Partially cover and simmer 10 minutes; add beans, tomatoes, and oregano
and simmer 5 minutes longer. Sprinkle each serving with cheese. Yield: 6
servings.

TOMATO BISQUE

2 (10¾-ounce) cans chicken
  broth, undiluted
1⅓ cups canned whole
  tomatoes
1 cup chopped celery
2 teaspoons chopped onion
1 cup chopped carrots
1 teaspoon salt, divided
6 tablespoons butter or
  margarine, divided

¼ cup all-purpose flour
2⅔ cups half-and-half,
  scalded
2 large tomatoes, peeled and
  chopped
2 tablespoons sugar
¼ teaspoon soda
Paprika

Combine broth, canned tomatoes, celery, onion, carrots, and ½ teaspoon salt in a saucepan. Heat to boiling point; reduce heat and simmer 20 minutes. Strain; reserve broth and discard the vegetables.

Melt 3 tablespoons butter in a saucepan; gradually stir in flour. Cook, stirring constantly, over low heat 2 minutes. Gradually add half-and-half, stirring constantly. Cook, stirring constantly, until thickened. Remove from heat; stir in reserved broth. Set aside and keep warm.

Melt remaining 3 tablespoons butter in a skillet. Add fresh tomato; sauté 2 to 4 minutes. Stir in sugar, remaining ½ teaspoon salt, and soda. Add to broth mixture, stirring well. Garnish with paprika. Yield: about 8 servings.

CURRIED TOMATO BISQUE

¼ cup finely sliced green
  onion
2 tablespoons melted butter
2 (10¾-ounce) cans
  condensed tomato soup,
  undiluted

2½ cups water
½ to ¾ teaspoon curry
  powder
2 hard-cooked egg yolks,
  grated

Sauté green onion in butter in saucepan until lightly browned. Add soup, water, and curry powder to taste. Heat, stirring constantly. Serve hot or chilled. Garnish with egg yolks. Yield: 4 to 6 servings.

Photograph for this recipe on page 130

CHILLED TOMATO-CHEESE SOUP

1 (10¾-ounce) can condensed
  cream of tomato soup,
  undiluted
2 cups half-and-half
1 teaspoon prepared
  horseradish
Few dashes of hot sauce

1 teaspoon lemon juice
½ cup cream-style cottage
  cheese
½ teaspoon salt
Dash of pepper
Chopped green onion tops or
  chives

Combine tomato soup, half-and-half, horseradish, hot sauce, and lemon juice; heat until well blended. Stir in cottage cheese, salt, and pepper; chill. Ladle into chilled bowls; sprinkle with green onion tops or chives. Yield: 4 to 6 servings.

GAZPACHO

½ cup diced celery
½ cup diced green pepper
½ cup diced onion
½ cup thinly sliced cucumber
1 cup diced tomatoes
1 (10¾-ounce) can tomato
   soup, undiluted
1 soup can water
1½ cups cocktail vegetable
   juice

1 tablespoon wine vinegar
1 tablespoon commercial
   Italian dressing
Garlic salt to taste
¼ teaspoon salt
⅛ teaspoon pepper
4 dashes of hot sauce
Dash of Worcestershire sauce

Combine all ingredients in a large bowl. Cover and refrigerate at least 4 hours. Stir gently. Serve in chilled bowls or mugs. Yield: 6 to 8 servings.

Photograph for this recipe on page 147

CHILLED SUMMER GAZPACHO

1 (2½-ounce) envelope tomato
   vegetable soup with
   noodles mix
3 cups water
1 cup tomato juice
2 cucumbers, peeled and
   chopped

2 cups bread cubes
¼ cup olive oil
¼ cup wine vinegar
1 clove garlic, minced
Bread cubes, chopped onion,
   cucumber, and green
   pepper

Cook soup in large saucepan according to package directions using water and tomato juice. Add cucumbers, 2 cups bread cubes, oil, vinegar, and garlic; puree in blender. Chill thoroughly. Serve bread cubes, chopped onion, chopped cucumber, and chopped green pepper as garnishes. Yield: 4 to 6 servings.

EASY GAZPACHO COOLER

3 tomatoes, quartered
1 clove garlic
½ small onion, sliced
½ green pepper, seeded and
   sliced
1 small cucumber, peeled and
   sliced

1 teaspoon salt
¼ teaspoon pepper
2 tablespoons olive oil
3 tablespoons wine vinegar
½ cup ice water
Toasted croutons or crackers

Combine all ingredients except croutons in blender. Cover and blend for 4 minutes on puree setting. Chill or pour into serving dishes with an ice cube in each dish. Serve with toasted croutons or crackers. Yield: 6 servings.

SPANISH GAZPACHO

1 large green pepper, seeded
and chopped, divided
2 cucumbers, peeled, seeded,
and chopped, divided
8 tomatoes, peeled and
mashed, divided
1 tablespoon salt
1½ teaspoons paprika
1 clove garlic, mashed

1 small, mild onion, peeled
and chopped
¼ cup olive oil
9 tablespoons wine vinegar
1½ cups cold tomato juice
Toasted croutons, chopped
cucumber, scallions, and
green pepper

Combine half the vegetables with salt and paprika. Vegetables must be
chopped extremely fine. Combine garlic, onion, oil, vinegar, and tomato
juice; put half into blender with half of vegetables. Process in blender until
vegetables are smoothly blended. Repeat the process with the remaining
chopped vegetables and remaining liquid. Combine the two batches. Chill
until very cold, but not so cold that the oil hardens. Taste for seasoning and
add more, if desired.

Pour into chilled bouillon cups. Serve with toasted croutons, chopped
cucumber, chopped scallions, and chopped green pepper. Yield: 8 servings.

CHEF'S FAVORITE SOUP

½ cup butter
4 large leeks, thinly sliced
3 stalks celery, thinly sliced
2 carrots, thinly sliced
6 tablespoons all-purpose flour
1 quart hot chicken or veal
broth (See Index)
2 cups shredded sharp
Cheddar cheese

3 cups whipping cream or
half-and-half
2 teaspoons salt
¼ teaspoon pepper
¼ cup chopped chives
½ teaspoon mace

Melt butter. Add vegetables; cook until brown. Blend in flour gradually.
Stir in hot broth and bring to a boil. Add cheese; stir until melted. Scald
cream and add to mixture. Season with salt and pepper. Simmer 20
minutes. Strain. Serve garnished with chives and mace. Yield: 8 to 10
servings.

CHEESE-VEGETABLE SOUP

2 large potatoes, peeled and
diced
1 cup chopped onion
½ cup finely chopped carrots
½ cup finely chopped celery
2 cups water

1 teaspoon salt, divided
1 quart chicken broth
1 cup half-and-half
White pepper to taste
3 cups shredded Cheddar
cheese

Cover vegetables with water in a large saucepan; add ½ teaspoon salt, and bring to a boil. Cover and simmer 15 minutes or until vegetables are tender; drain.

Combine vegetables, chicken broth, half-and-half, remaining salt, and pepper; heat thoroughly. Add cheese, stirring until melted. Serve immediately. Yield: 8 to 10 servings.

CHILLED SUMMER GARDEN SOUP

3 cups tomato juice	2 stalks celery, cut into
2 cups water	1-inch pieces
1 (1⅜-ounce) envelope onion	1 (8-ounce) carton commercial
soup mix	sour cream

Combine tomato juice, water, soup mix, and celery. Chill 1 to 2 hours. Strain; blend in sour cream. Yield: 6 servings.

GODDESS OF SPRING SOUP

1 (10¾-ounce) can condensed	½ bunch watercress
cream of potato soup,	2 cups torn lettuce
undiluted	1 cup milk
1 cup cold water	½ teaspoon salt
2 cups chicken broth (See	Dash of pepper
Index)	4 frankfurters, cut into ¼-inch
1 clove garlic	slices
1 leek or 3 green onions,	1 tablespoon butter
sliced	Watercress
2 cups spinach leaves	Croutons

Combine soup and water; add broth, garlic, and leek. Heat for 10 minutes; remove garlic clove. Add spinach, ½ bunch watercress, and lettuce. Simmer for 15 minutes. Drain off 1 cup broth, and reserve liquid. Place vegetables and remaining broth in blender or put through food mill. Blend until smooth; combine with reserved broth, milk, and seasonings. Reheat just to the boiling point. Sauté frankfurters in butter in a hot skillet; add to soup. Garnish with watercress and croutons. Yield: 6 to 8 servings.

EASY MINESTRONE

1 tablespoon olive oil	1 (1⅜-ounce) envelope onion
1 medium zucchini, diced	soup mix
1 medium tomato, cut up	¼ cup uncooked elbow
1 cup chick peas	macaroni
1 quart water	Dash of basil

Heat oil in large saucepan; cook zucchini, tomato, and chick peas for 5 minutes. Add water; bring to a boil. Stir in soup mix, elbow macaroni, and basil; cover and simmer for 10 minutes. Yield: 4 to 6 servings.

MINESTRONE

¼ pound lean salt pork, finely
  diced
2 quarts hot water
1½ cups tomato juice
2 (15-ounce) cans kidney
  beans
1 (11½-ounce) can bean with
  bacon soup, undiluted
6 beef bouillon cubes
1 cup diced carrot
1 cup chopped celery
1 cup shredded cabbage

1 cup chopped green onions
1 cup chopped spinach or ½
  package frozen chopped
  spinach
1 teaspoon sweet basil
1 teaspoon monosodium
  glutamate
½ teaspoon salt
½ teaspoon freshly ground
  pepper
¾ cup uncooked regular rice
Grated Parmesan cheese

Sauté salt pork in a deep saucepan until crisp and brown. Add remaining
ingredients except rice and cheese; bring to a boil. Cover and simmer over
low heat 1 hour, stirring occasionally. Add rice, and simmer an additional
30 minutes. Ladle into soup bowls, and sprinkle with cheese. Yield: 10
servings.

MINUTE MINESTRONE

1 (2½-ounce) envelope
   tomato-vegetable soup mix
   with noodles
3 cups boiling water
1 medium onion, chopped
1 (16-ounce) can red kidney
   beans

1 (12-ounce) can whole
   kernel corn
1 (8-ounce) can tomato sauce
1 teaspoon salt
⅛ teaspoon pepper
½ cup chopped parsley
Grated Parmesan cheese

Stir soup mix into boiling water in large saucepan; add onion, kidney beans, corn, tomato sauce, salt, and pepper. Cover and heat to boiling; cook 10 minutes or until onion is tender. Stir in parsley. Serve in mugs or bowls with a generous sprinkling of Parmesan cheese. Yield: 4 to 6 servings.

QUICK MINESTRA

3 ounces cooked ham fat,
   diced
1 small onion, diced
1 (16-ounce) can lima beans

1 (16-ounce) can spinach or
   kale
Salt and pepper to taste

In electric blender, combine ham fat and onion. Mince, but do not puree. Put mixture into heavy saucepan. Add lima beans. Run a sharp knife down through the can of spinach or kale to cut it up; add to pan. Simmer 20 to 30 minutes. Season. Yield: 4 servings.

MULLIGATAWNY SOUP

1 cup finely chopped onion
3 tablespoons butter
1 cup all-purpose flour
½ tablespoon curry powder
2 quarts chicken broth
2 apples

½ cup shredded coconut
1 cup whipping cream
1 cup diced eggplant
1 tablespoon butter
Salt and pepper to taste

In a heavy skillet sauté onion in 3 tablespoons butter over medium heat until brown. Add flour and simmer 20 minutes. Add curry powder, mixing well. (Some people like hot food; if you do not, use ¼ to ½ teaspoon curry powder.) Add broth and bring to a boil. Peel and dice apples; reserve the peelings. Add coconut and apple peelings to broth and allow soup to simmer for 1 hour. Strain. Bring to a boil again and add cream and diced apples. Sauté eggplant in 1 tablespoon butter over medium heat and add to cooked broth; add salt and pepper. Yield: 10 to 12 servings.

PEPPER POT SOUP

Bones from beef or veal
¼ pound tripe, cubed
1½ quarts water
½ bay leaf
1½ teaspoons salt
½ teaspoon pepper
3 onions, diced and divided

2 potatoes, diced
2 carrots, diced
¼ cup diced celery
½ green pepper, diced
2 tablespoons salad oil
Dash of cayenne pepper
2 tablespoons minced parsley

Simmer bones and tripe for 2 hours in water with bay leaf, salt, pepper, and 1 onion. Cook remaining onions, potatoes, carrots, celery, and green pepper in oil for 10 minutes; do not brown. Remove bones from broth; add vegetables and cayenne pepper. Add more salt and black pepper, if needed. Simmer for 30 minutes; add parsley. Yield: 6 to 8 servings.

SALAD SOUP

1 (46-ounce) can tomato juice
1 tablespoon lemon juice
1 teaspoon Worcestershire
    sauce
1 tablespoon olive oil
1 teaspoon onion salt
½ teaspoon celery salt
½ cup finely chopped green
    onion

½ cup finely chopped
    cucumber
½ cup finely chopped green
    pepper
½ cup finely chopped celery
½ cup finely chopped carrot

Combine all ingredients, mixing well. Refrigerate, covered, at least 24 hours. Serve cold. Yield: 6 to 8 servings.

VEGETABLE SOUP

3 slices bacon, chopped
1 pound lean beef stew meat
½ pound soup bone
3 tablespoons salad oil,
    divided
½ cup chopped onion
½ cup chopped celery
1 cup diced carrot
¼ cup chopped green pepper
1 cup diced potato
1 quart water or broth

1 teaspoon salt
½ teaspoon pepper
1 (8½-ounce) can green peas
1 (8¾-ounce) can whole
    kernel corn
1 (8-ounce) can tomato
    wedges
½ cup uncooked macaroni
2 tablespoons chopped parsley
1 cup shredded cabbage

Brown meat and bone in 2 tablespoons salad oil in Dutch oven. Sauté onion, celery, carrot, green pepper, and potato in 1 tablespoon salad oil in heavy skillet until slightly brown. Add water or broth to meat and bring to a boil. Simmer 20 minutes. Add sautéed vegetables and seasonings, peas, corn, and tomatoes and simmer 30 minutes. Add macaroni and simmer 30 minutes longer, adding parsley and cabbage the last 10 minutes. Yield: 6 to 8 servings.

CREAM OF VEGETABLE SOUP

2 tablespoons butter	1 cup diced, cooked potato
½ cup minced onion	½ cup cooked green peas
3 tablespoons all-purpose flour	2 tablespoons minced parsley
2 teaspoons salt	1 teaspoon Worcestershire
⅛ teaspoon pepper	sauce
1 quart milk	Dash of cayenne pepper
¼ cup minced, cooked carrot	¼ cup shredded pasteurized
¼ cup diced, cooked celery	process American cheese

Melt butter over low heat; add onion and sauté until tender. Add flour and seasonings and blend. Add milk, stirring constantly until smooth and thickened. Add vegetables, parsley, Worcestershire sauce, and cayenne pepper. Heat; sprinkle top with cheese. Serve at once. Yield: 6 servings.

HEARTY VEGETABLE SOUP

1½ pounds stew meat, cut into 1-inch cubes	4 cups shredded cabbage
3 quarts water, divided	2 (28-ounce) cans whole tomatoes, undrained
2½ tablespoons salt, divided	1 teaspoon sugar
½ teaspoon pepper	1 (17-ounce) can whole kernel corn, undrained
Celery leaves	1 (8¾-ounce) can whole kernel corn, undrained
2 large onions, chopped and divided	1 (10-ounce) package frozen green peas
2 bay leaves, crushed	1 (10-ounce) package frozen lima beans
¼ teaspoon oregano	
¼ teaspoon thyme	
1½ cups diced potato	
1 cup diced carrot	
½ pound green beans, cut into 1½-inch pieces	

Place meat in soup kettle with 2½ quarts water. Add 1 tablespoon salt, pepper, celery leaves, and 1 chopped onion. Combine bay leaves, oregano, and thyme; tie in cheesecloth bag and drop into kettle with meat. Cover and simmer for at least 3 hours. Remove celery leaves. Remove meat from bones, cut into bite-size pieces, and add to stock. Add potato, carrot, green beans, cabbage, 1 chopped onion, and 1 tablespoon salt; simmer for 1 hour.

Add 2 cups water, tomatoes, sugar, corn, peas, lima beans, and ½ tablespoon salt. Cook an additional hour. Remove cheesecloth spice bag before serving. Yield: 25 to 30 servings.

GARDEN-FRESH VEGETABLE SOUP

¼ cup olive oil
2 onions, thinly sliced
2 cloves garlic, finely chopped
1 (about 1½ cups) small
   eggplant, peeled and cubed
2 medium zucchini, sliced
1 green pepper, diced
1 (28-ounce) can whole
   tomatoes

1 quart chicken broth (See
   Index)
1½ teaspoons basil
½ teaspoon ground coriander
Salt and freshly ground black
   pepper to taste
4 ounces small-shell
   macaroni, cooked and
   drained

Heat oil in a heavy kettle and sauté onions and garlic until tender and golden. Add eggplant, zucchini, and green pepper and cook, stirring over medium heat, until lightly browned, about 8 to 10 minutes. Add remaining ingredients except macaroni. Bring to a boil, cover, and simmer 10 minutes or until vegetables are barely tender. Add macaroni and simmer 4 minutes longer. Yield: 6 servings.

OLD-FASHIONED VEGETABLE SOUP

1½ pounds soup bone with
   meat
1½ pounds lean brisket, cut
   into cubes
3 stalks celery, chopped
3 large carrots, chopped
2 medium onions, chopped
1 (28-ounce) can whole
   tomatoes, undrained

½ teaspoon basil
½ teaspoon thyme
½ teaspoon marjoram
½ cup chopped parsley
1½ teaspoons salt
½ teaspoon pepper
2 cups green lima beans
1 cup cut corn
1 cup green peas

Put soup bone and cubed meat into a large kettle; cover with water and bring to a boil. Add chopped celery, carrots, and onions. Stir in tomatoes, basil, thyme, marjoram, parsley, salt, and pepper. Cover and cook over low heat for 3 to 5 hours. About 30 minutes before serving, add lima beans, corn, and peas; cook until heated thoroughly. Serve hot. Yield: 8 servings.

QUICK VEGETABLE SOUP

2 cups hot water
4 beef bouillon cubes
1½ teaspoons salt
¼ teaspoon pepper
1 (10-ounce) package frozen
   peas and carrots, thawed

1 (10-ounce) package frozen
   green beans, thawed
2 cups canned whole tomatoes
1 tablespoon dry onion flakes

Place all ingredients in saucepan. Cover and cook on high heat until steaming; lower heat and cook for 10 minutes. Yield: 6 servings.

VEGETABLE SOUP WITH MACARONI

1 pound ground beef
1 clove garlic, minced
1 cup chopped onion
2 cups coarsely cut cabbage
1 (16-ounce) can mixed
  vegetables, undrained
1 (28-ounce) can whole
  tomatoes, undrained

2½ teaspoons salt
¼ teaspoon pepper
3 cups water
1 cup shell macaroni,
  uncooked
½ cup grated Parmesan
  cheese

Brown ground beef. Add remaining ingredients except macaroni and Parmesan cheese; bring to a boil. Add macaroni and simmer for 15 minutes or until macaroni is tender. Remove from heat. Sprinkle each serving with Parmesan cheese. Yield: 8 servings.

BEEFY VEGETABLE SOUP

2 pounds ground beef
1 cup all-purpose flour
½ cup melted margarine
2 quarts water
1 cup chopped onion
1 cup chopped carrots
1 cup chopped celery
1 (10-ounce) package frozen
  mixed vegetables

1 (28-ounce) can whole
  tomatoes
2 tablespoons beef-flavored
  instant bouillon
1 tablespoon Ac'cent
2 to 3 tablespoons pepper

Cook ground beef until done, stirring to crumble. Drain on paper towels; discard pan drippings.
  Stir flour into margarine in a Dutch oven; cook over low heat 3 to 5 minutes, stirring constantly, until a smooth paste is formed. Gradually stir in water; cook, stirring constantly, until bubbly. Stir in cooked ground beef and remaining ingredients. Bring soup to a boil; cover and simmer 45 minutes to 1 hour. Yield: 6 to 8 servings.

VEGETABLE MEATBALL SOUP

½ pound ground beef
1 egg
1 cup soft breadcrumbs
½ teaspoon salt
Dash of pepper
Dash of oregano
Dash of garlic powder
1 tablespoon butter or
   margarine

1 (2-ounce) envelope country
   vegetable beef soup mix
   with noodles
3 cups water
1 (16-ounce) can whole
   tomatoes, coarsely chopped

Combine ground beef, egg, breadcrumbs, salt, pepper, oregano, and garlic powder in small bowl; blend well. Shape into about 20 marble-size meatballs.

Melt butter in medium-size skillet and cook meatballs until lightly browned; drain off excess fat. Add soup mix to meatballs in skillet; blend in water and tomatoes. Bring to a boil, stirring occasionally. Partially cover and simmer 15 minutes. Yield: 6 servings.

VEGETABLE AND MEATBALL SOUP

1½ quarts water	2 teaspoons seasoned pepper
4 cups canned tomatoes	2 teaspoons ground basil
1½ cups chopped celery	2 pounds ground beef
2 cups sliced carrots	2 eggs
5 medium potatoes, peeled and diced	⅓ cup cracker crumbs
2 large onions, chopped	2 tablespoons milk
4 teaspoons salt	2 teaspoons seasoned salt
3 bay leaves	Dash of pepper
2 tablespoons chopped parsley	2 (16-ounce) cans cut green beans
1 tablespoon sugar	1 (12-ounce) can whole kernel corn
2 teaspoons ground oregano	

Combine first 13 ingredients in a large Dutch oven; cover and bring mixture to a boil.

Combine ground beef, eggs, cracker crumbs, milk, seasoned salt, and pepper; mix well, and shape into 1-inch balls. Drop meatballs into boiling soup, and simmer 30 minutes. Add beans and corn during last 10 minutes of cooking time. Soup may be frozen for later use. Yield: 12 to 15 servings.

Photograph for this recipe on page facing

MEXICAN VEGETABLE SOUP

1 whole chicken breast, split	1 (7-ounce) can whole kernel corn, drained
2 quarts water	¼ cup chopped onion
1 medium onion, sliced	⅓ cup tomato puree
1 tablespoon salt	2 avocados, sliced
Dash of pepper	1 (3-ounce) package cream cheese, diced
1 tablespoon shortening	
2 cups chopped zucchini	

Cook chicken in water with onion, salt, and pepper for 1 hour or until chicken is tender. Remove chicken; bone and dice. Reserve broth.

Melt shortening in medium-size skillet; cook zucchini, corn, onion, and tomato puree for 5 minutes. Add to broth; cover and simmer for an additional 20 minutes. Before serving, add chicken, avocado, and cream cheese. Yield: 8 to 10 servings.

SOUTHERN VEGETABLE SOUP

1 pound boneless chuck roast cut into 1-inch squares
3 tablespoons butter
1 (1- to 1½-pound) beef shank or knuckle bone or 1 leftover rump bone of rare roast beef or 1 leg of lamb bone or bone from a large sirloin steak
5 quarts water
3 red or green hot peppers
3 medium onions, each cut into tenths
4 stalks celery, finely chopped
3 carrots, cut into small rings
1 teaspoon dried green onion
6 tomatoes
1 (16-ounce) can whole tomatoes
1 tablespoon plus two teaspoons salt
2 teaspoons seasoned salt
1 medium Irish potato, diced
1 quart fresh butterbeans or 1 quart small frozen green limas
8 ears fresh corn cut from the cob or 1 quart frozen corn
1 quart fresh okra, cut up, or 1 (10-ounce) package frozen cut-up okra
1 tablespoon Worcestershire sauce
½ tablespoon salt (optional)

Brown boneless beef chuck in butter in a heavy skillet over medium heat. Rinse out skillet with some of the water, and pour rinsings into large Dutch oven or soup kettle. Add bone, browned beef, water, seasonings, and vegetables listed up through the diced potato. Bring to a boil and let cook for 1 hour on medium heat. Arrange cover so that steam may escape. If cholesterol is a problem in your diet, cook these first ingredients, cool and refrigerate. The next morning, remove the congealed fat with a spoon. Resume preparation by adding butterbeans and cooking for 30 minutes. Add corn and let soup simmer 30 minutes more. Add okra and Worcestershire sauce and cook an additional 30 minutes. Taste and gradually add ½ tablespoon salt, if desired. Remove hot peppers when desired zip pleases your taste. Soup requires no thickening; it has plenty of body. Should you like it even thicker, add 2 tablespoons flour to 1 cup cold water and stir gradually into soup. Allow soup to cool completely before freezing. Yield: 3½ gallons.

PRINCE AND PAUPER VEGETABLE SOUP

1 pound meaty beef bones
Salt and pepper to taste
¼ teaspoon chili powder
¼ teaspoon Worcestershire sauce
⅛ teaspoon hot sauce
1 (16-ounce) can stewed tomatoes
1 large onion, chopped
3 stalks celery, chopped
3 carrots, chopped
2 cups shredded cabbage
1 small turnip, chopped
1 (8-ounce) can whole kernel corn, drained
½ (10-ounce) package frozen okra
¼ cup red wine

Combine beef bones, salt, pepper, chili powder, Worcestershire sauce, and hot sauce in a large saucepan; add water to cover. Place over heat; cover and simmer for 1 hour.

Add tomatoes, onion, and celery; cook for 1 hour. Add carrots, cabbage, and turnip; continue to cook over low heat for 1 hour. Add remaining ingredients and cook for 30 minutes. Yield: 10 servings.

TUNA VEGETABLE SOUP

1 (6½- or 7-ounce) can tuna
   fish
½ cup chopped celery
½ cup chopped onion
1 cup diced potato
1 cup water
1½ teaspoons salt
¼ teaspoon thyme

Dash of cayenne pepper
1 (10½-ounce) can tomato
   puree
1½ cups water
1 (8-ounce) can whole kernel
   corn, undrained
2 teaspoons sugar

Drain tuna fish, reserving 2 tablespoons oil; break into large pieces. Cook celery and onion in oil until tender. Add potato, water, and seasoning. Cover and cook about 15 minutes or until potato is tender. Add tuna fish and remaining ingredients; heat. Yield: 6 servings.

TURKEY-VEGETABLE SOUP MATE

1 (10¾-ounce) can condensed
    turkey vegetable soup,
    undiluted
1 (10¾-ounce) can condensed
    tomato soup, undiluted

2 soup cans water
Cereal bits, croutons, or sour
    cream and chives

Combine all ingredients in a saucepan. Heat, stirring now and then.
Garnish with cereal bits, croutons, or sour cream sprinkled with chives.
Yield: 4 to 6 servings.

appendices

Because soups are so often a part of a larger meal, the Foods Editors of *Southern Living* have included information they find is helpful in preparing all types of dishes. We hope that you will find the following charts useful in your culinary endeavors.

Handy Substitutions

Even the best of cooks occasionally runs out of an ingredient she needs and is unable to stop what she is doing to go to the store. At times like those, sometimes another ingredient or combination of ingredients can be used. Here is a list of substitutions and equivalents that yield satisfactory results in most cases.

Ingredient called for	Substitution
1 cup self-rising flour	1 cup all-purpose flour plus 1 teaspoon baking powder and ½ teaspoon salt
1 cup cake flour	1 cup sifted all-purpose flour minus 2 tablespoons
1 cup all-purpose flour	1 cup cake flour plus 2 tablespoons
1 teaspoon baking powder	½ teaspoon cream of tartar plus ¼ teaspoon soda
1 tablespoon cornstarch or arrowroot	2 tablespoons all-purpose flour
1 tablespoon tapioca	1½ tablespoons all-purpose flour
2 large eggs	3 small eggs
1 egg	2 egg yolks (for custard)
1 egg	2 egg yolks plus 1 tablespoon water (for cookies)
1 cup commercial sour cream	1 tablespoon lemon juice plus evaporated milk to equal 1 cup; or 3 tablespoons butter plus ⅞ cup sour milk
1 cup yogurt	1 cup buttermilk or sour milk
1 cup sour milk or buttermilk	1 tablespoon vinegar or lemon juice plus sweet milk to equal 1 cup
1 cup fresh milk	½ cup evaporated milk plus ½ cup water

Handy Substitutions (Continued)

Ingredient called for	Substitution
1 cup fresh milk	3 to 5 tablespoons nonfat dry milk solids in 1 cup water
1 cup honey	1¼ cups sugar plus ¼ cup liquid
1 square (1 ounce) unsweetened chocolate	3 tablespoons cocoa plus 1 tablespoon butter or margarine
1 clove fresh garlic	1 teaspoon garlic salt or ⅛ teaspoon garlic powder
1 teaspoon onion powder	2 teaspoons minced onion
1 tablespoon fresh herbs	1 teaspoon ground or crushed dry herbs
¼ cup chopped fresh parsley	1 tablespoon dehydrated parsley
1 teaspoon dry mustard	1 tablespoon prepared mustard
1 pound fresh mushrooms	6 ounces canned mushrooms

Equivalent Weights and Measures

Food	Weight or Count	Measure
Apples	1 pound (3 medium)	3 cups, sliced
Bacon	8 slices cooked	½ cup, crumbled
Bananas	1 pound (3 medium)	2½ cups, sliced, or about 2 cups, mashed
Bread	1 pound	12 to 16 slices
Bread	About 1½ slices	1 cup soft crumbs
Butter or margarine	1 pound	2 cups
Butter or margarine	¼-pound stick	½ cup
Butter or margarine	Size of an egg	About ¼ cup
Candied fruit or peels	½ pound	1¼ cups, cut
Cheese, American	1 pound	4 to 5 cups, shredded
cottage	1 pound	2 cups
cream	3-pound package	6 tablespoons
Chocolate morsels	6-ounce package	1 cup
Cocoa	1 pound	4 cups
Coconut, flaked or shredded	1 pound	5 cups
Coffee	1 pound	80 tablespoons
Cornmeal	1 pound	3 cups
Cream, heavy or whipping	½ pint	2 cups, whipped
Dates, pitted	1 pound	2 to 3 cups, chopped
Dates, pitted	7¼-ounce package	1¼ cups, chopped
Eggs	5 large	About 1 cup
Eggs whites	8 large	About 1 cup
Egg yolks	12 large	About 1 cup
Flour		
all-purpose	1 pound	4 cups, sifted
cake	1 pound	4¾ to 5 cups, sifted
whole wheat	1 pound	3½ cups, unsifted
Graham crackers	16 to 18 crackers	1⅓ cups crumbs
Lemon juice	1 medium	2 to 3 tablespoons
Lemon rind	1 medium	2 teaspoons, grated
Macaroni	4 ounces (1 cup)	2¼ cups, cooked
Milk		
evaporated	6-ounce can	¾ cup
evaporated	14½-ounce can	1⅔ cups
sweetened condensed	14-ounce can	1¼ cups
sweetened condensed	15-ounce can	1⅓ cups
Miniature marshmallows	½ pound	4½ cups
Nuts, in shell		
almonds	1 pound	1 to 1¾ cups nutmeats
peanuts	1 pound	2 cups nutmeats
pecans	1 pound	2¼ cups nutmeats
walnuts	1 pound	1⅔ cups nutmeats

Equivalent Weights and Measures

Food	Weight or Count	Measure
Nuts, shelled		
almonds	1 pound, 2 ounces	4 cups
peanuts	1 pound	4 cups
pecans	1 pound	4 cups
walnuts	1 pound	3 cups
Orange, juice	1 medium	⅓ cup
Orange, rind	1 medium	2 tablespoons, grated
Potatoes	2 pounds	6 medium
Potatoes	4 to 5 medium	4 cups, cooked and cubed
Raisins, seedless	1 pound	3 cups
Rice	1 cup	About 4 cups, cooked
Spaghetti	7 ounces	About 4 cups, cooked
Sugar		
brown	1 pound	2¼ cups, firmly packed
powdered	1 pound	3½ cups, unsifted
granulated	1 pound	2 cups
Whipping cream	1 cup	2 cups, whipped

Equivalent Measurements

Use standard measuring cups (both dry and liquid measure) and measuring spoons when measuring ingredients. All measurements given below are level.

3 teaspoons	1 tablespoon
4 tablespoons	¼ cup
5⅓ tablespoons	⅓ cup
8 tablespoons	½ cup
16 tablespoons	1 cup
2 tablespoons (liquid)	1 ounce
1 cup	8 fluid ounces
2 cups	1 pint (16 fluid ounces)
4 cups	1 quart
4 quarts	1 gallon
⅛ cup	2 tablespoons
⅓ cup	5 tablespoons plus 1 teaspoon
⅔ cup	10 tablespoons plus 2 teaspoons
¾ cup	12 tablespoons
Few grains (or dash)	Less than ⅛ teaspoon
Pinch	As much as can be taken between tip of finger and thumb

Metric Measures

Approximate Conversion to Metric Measures			
When you know . . .	Multiply by . . . Mass (weight)	To find . . .	Symbol
ounces	28	grams	g
pounds	0.45	kilograms	kg
	Volume		
teaspoons	5	milliliters	ml
tablespoons	15	milliliters	ml
fluid ounces	30	milliliters	ml
cups	0.24	liters	l
pints	0.47	liters	l
quarts	0.95	liters	l
gallons	3.8	liters	l

Cooking Measure Equivalents					
Metric Cup	Volume (Liquid)	Liquid Solids (Butter)	Fine Powder (Flour)	Granular (Sugar)	Grain (Rice)
1	250 ml	200 g	140 g	190 g	150 g
¾	188 ml	150 g	105 g	143 g	113 g
⅔	167 ml	133 g	93 g	127 g	100 g
½	125 ml	100 g	70 g	95 g	75 g
⅓	83 ml	67 g	47 g	63 g	50 g
¼	63 ml	50 g	35 g	48 g	38 g
⅛	31 ml	25 g	18 g	24 g	19 g

SPICE CHART

For: / Use:	Appetizers & Garnishes	Fish	Eggs or Cheese	Meats	Poultry & Game	Vegetables	Sauces	Desserts & Beverages
Allspice		*Marinades		Pot Roast, Stew, Braised Veal, Pork, Lamb	*Marinades (for Game)	*Pickling liquids for all vegetables	Chili, Catsup, Barbecue, Spaghetti, Brown	Apple Pie, Pumpkin Pie
Beau Monde Seasoning	Dips, Spreads	Broiled, Baked	All Egg Dishes	Steaks, Chops, Roasts	Chicken, Duck, Turkey		White, Tomato, Barbecue	
Cardamom				Spareribs, Ham, Pork			Barbecue	Coffee Cakes, Breads, Fruitcake, Cookies; Hot Fruit Punches, *Mulled Wines
Chili Con Carne Seasoning	Cheese Dips, Spreads		Welsh Rarebit, Soufflés, Baked or Scrambled Eggs	Marinades for Pork, Lamb, Beef	Marinades for Chicken	Corn, Rice, Kidney, Pink or Lima Beans	Barbecue, Cheese	
Cinnamon	Cranberry Sauce, Pickled or Spiced Fruits, Broiled Grapefruit, *Pickles, *Chutney, Catsup	*Court Bouillon for all Fish and Shellfish		Ham, Lamb, Pork Chops, Beef Stews, *Stock for Pickled or Smoked Meats	Dressing for Goose			All Milk Drinks, Custard, Fruit or Rice Puddings, Pumpkin, Apple, Peach, Cream or Custard Pies; *Mulled Wine, *Hot Tea, *Coffee, *Chocolate, *Spiced and Pickled Fruits
Cloves		*Court Bouillon, Baked Fish	Scrambled or Creamed Eggs	*Marinades for Beef, Pork, Lamb, Veal, *Stock for Boiling Meat Loaf	*Marinades for Game, *Stock for Boiling Poultry	Harvard Beets, Sweet Potatoes, Tomatoes	Spaghetti, Chili, Wine, Barbecue	*Hot or Cold Fruit Punches, *Mulled Wines; All spice cakes, cookies, and puddings
Curry Powder	Dips	Broiled, Baked	Deviled Eggs, Egg Salad, Cheese Spreads	Lamb, Pork, Beef	Chicken	Cooked Vegetables	Curry, Marinades for Lamb, Beef, Chicken, Fish, Game, White Sauce	
Ginger	*Pickled or Spiced Fruits, *Preserves, Jams, Jellies	Broiled, Baked		Pot Roast, Steak, Lamb, *Marinades for Beef, Lamb	Dressing for Poultry, *Marinades for Chicken, Turkey	Candied Sweet Potatoes, Glazed Carrots or Onions, Winter Squash	For Pork, Veal, Fish	Canned Fruit, Gingerbread, Gingersnaps, Ginger Cookies; Steamed Puddings, Bread or Rice Puddings

For:	Appetizers & Garnishes	Fish	Eggs or Cheese	Meats	Poultry & Game	Vegetables	Sauces	Desserts & Beverages
Use: **Mace**	Pickles Fruit Preserves Jellies	Trout Scalloped Fish	Welsh Rarebit	Lamb Chops Sausage		Buttered Carrots Cauliflower Squash Swiss Chard Spinach Mashed or Creamed Potatoes	Fish Veal Chicken	Cooked Apples Cherries Prunes Apricots Pancakes Chocolate Pudding	Fruit Cottage or Custard Puddings
Mustard (Hot)	Butter for Vegetables Seafood Cocktail	Crab		Stew Pot Roast Ham Pork	Fried Chicken	Creamed Asparagus Broccoli Brussels Sprouts Cabbage Celery Green Beans Pickled Beets	French Dressing Mustard Sauce Gravies Cream Cheese and Newburg Sauces	
Mustard (Mild)		Fried Broiled		Beef Stew Swiss Steak		Scalloped & Au Gratin Potatoes Steamed Cabbage Brussels Sprouts Asparagus Broccoli	French Dressing Cooked Salad Dressing Mayonnaise Raisin, White Sauces	
Nutmeg	Garnish for milk, chocolate, and spiced drinks	Baked Croquettes Broiled	Welsh Rarebit	Swedish Meat Balls Meat Loaf Meat Pie	Chicken	Glazed Carrots Cauliflower Squash Swiss Chard Spinach	White Sauce for Chicken Seafood Veal	Ice Cream Cakes	Cookies Puddings
Paprika	Pâtés Canapes Hors d'oeuvres		All Cheese Mixtures	Ground Beef Dipping Mixture for Pork Chops Veal Cutlets	Dipping Mixture for Fried Chicken	Baked Potatoes	Cooked French Sour Cream Salad Dressings White Sauce	
Tumeric		Marinades for Broiled Salmon, Lobster, or Shrimp	Scrambled or Creamed Eggs	Curried Beef or Lamb	Marinades for Chicken		White Mustard	
Vanilla Beans							Fruit	Ice Cream Cakes	Custards Puddings

Note: All spices are ground except those indicated by an asterisk (*), which indicates whole spice

Courtesy of Spice Islands

HERB CHART

For: Use:	Appetizers & Garnishes	Soups	Fish	Eggs or Cheese	Meats	Poultry & Game	Vegetables	Salads	Sauces
Basil	Tomato Juice Seafood Cocktail	Tomato Chowders Spinach Minestrone	Shrimps Broiled Fish	Scrambled Eggs Cream Cheese Welsh Rarebit	Liver Lamb Sausage	Venison Duck	Eggplant Squash Tomatoes Onions	Tomato Seafood Chicken	Tomato Spaghetti Orange (for Game) Butter (for Fish)
Bay Leaves	Tomato Juice Aspic	Stock Bean	Court Bouillon Poached Halibut Salmon		Stews Pot Roast Shish Kabob Tripe	Chicken Fricassee Stews	Tomatoes	Aspic Marinades for Beet Onion	All Marinades Espagnole Champagne
Dillweed	Cheese Dips Seafood Spreads Pickles	Borscht Tomato Chicken	Halibut Shrimp Sole	Omelet Cottage Cheese	Beef Sweetbreads Veal Lamb	Chicken Pie Creamed Chicken	Cabbage Beets Beans Celery	Coleslaw Cucumber Potato	White (for Fish) Tartare
Fines Herbs			Baked or Broiled Cod or Halibut Dressings	Omelet Scrambled Eggs Cheese Sauce Soufflés	Broiled Liver and Kidneys Roast Pork Pot Roast, Stews Meat Loaf Hamburgers	Dressings Broiled Chicken	Peas Mushrooms Tomatoes		
Marjoram	Liver Pâté Stuffed Mushrooms Butters	Spinach Clam Mock Turtle Onion	Crab, Tuna Clams Halibut Salmon	Omelet Scrambled Eggs	Pot Roast Pork Beef Veal	Creamed Chicken Dressings Goose	Carrots Zucchini Peas	Chicken Mixed Green	White Brown Sour Cream
Oregano	Guacamole Tomato	Tomato Bean Minestrone	Shrimp Clams Lobster	Huevos Rancheros	Sausage Lamb Meat Loaf	Marinades Dressings Pheasant Guinea Hen	Tomatoes Cabbage Lentils Broccoli	Vegetable Bean Tomato	Spaghetti Tomato

HERB CHART — Continued

For:	Appetizers & Garnishes	Soups	Fish	Eggs or Cheese	Meats	Poultry & Game	Vegetables	Salads	Sauces
Peppermint*	Fruit Cup Melon Balls Cranberry Juice	Pea	Garnish for Broiled Shrimps Prawns	Cream Cheese	Lamb Veal		Carrots New Potatoes Spinach Zucchini	Fruit Coleslaw Orange Pear	Mint
Rosemary	Fruit Cup	Turtle, Pea Spinach Chicken	Salmon Halibut	Omelet Scrambled Eggs	Lamb, Veal Beef Ham Loaf	Partridge Capon, Duck Rabbit	Peas Spinach Potatoes	Fruit	White Barbecue Tomato
Saffron		Bouillabaisse Chicken, Turkey	Halibut Sole	Cream Cheese Scrambled Eggs	Veal	Chicken Rabbit	Risotto Rice	Seafood Chicken	Fish Sauce
Sage	Sharp Cheese Spreads	Chicken Chowders	Halibut Salmon	Cheddar Cottage	Stews Pork Sausage	Goose Turkey Rabbit Dressings	Lima Beans Eggplant Onions Tomatoes		
Salad Herbs	Fruit Cup Vegetable and Tomato Juices Seafood Cocktail Sauce		All Fish		Meat Loaf			All Salads	
Savory	Vegetable Juice Cocktail	Lentil Bean Vegetable	Crab Salmon	Scrambled or Deviled Eggs	Pork Veal	Chicken Dressings	Beans, Rice Lentils Sauerkraut	Mixed Green String Bean Potato	Horseradish Fish Sauce
Tarragon	Tomato Juice Cheese Spreads Liver Pâtés	Chicken Mushroom Tomato Pea	All Fish	All Egg Dishes	Veal Sweetbreads Yorkshire Pudding	Chicken Squab Duck	Salsify Celery Root Mushrooms	Mixed Green Chicken Fruit Seafood	Bearnaise Tartare Verte Mustard
Thyme	Tomato Juice Fish Spreads Cocktails	Borscht Gumbo, Pea Clam Chowder Vegetable	Tuna Scallops Crab Sole	Shirred Eggs Cottage Cheese	Mutton Meat Loaf Veal Liver	Dressings Venison Fricassee Pheasant	Onions Carrots Beets	Beet Tomato Aspics	Creole Espagnole Herb Bouquets

*Use ½ teaspoon for 6 servings

Courtesy of Spice Islands

INDEX